Advanced praise for *The S*

The Science of Mother-Infant Sleep: Current Findings on Bedsharing, Breastfeeding, Sleep Training, and Normal Sleep is about much more than sleep—and, yes, a new parent must read this collection for understanding about sleep—but it's also about how we spend our time awake and in love with our children. *The Science of Mother-Infant Sleep* goes deep, to the stressors and situations that we recognize as traumatic with a capital T, but also to the trauma that we have normalized and don't recognize—the coping through controlling, defensiveness, lack of connection, and even diet. It is the chronic, socially acceptable trauma that also merits our attention, and our commitment to healthy alternatives and support. AP-practicing parents will find support and encouragement. API Support Group Leaders will share it with their questioning parents to guide their understanding about API's Principle of engaging in safe sleep, physically and emotionally, and how their infant settles through proximity and responsiveness. A grateful thank you to the contributors.

—Samantha Gray
Executive Director, *Attachment Parenting International:
Nurturing Children for a Compassionate World*

Finally! *The Science of Mother Infant Sleep* is the only practitioner and parent-friendly resource for everyone interested in thoughtful, thorough, and rational discussion of mother-infant sleep studies and crying-it-out strategies.While the infant sleep debate rages on, this book offers reasonable and reassuring recommendations that maintain safety and the integrity of the mother-baby relationship.

—Lysa Parker, MS, CFLE
Coauthor, *Attached at the Heart: Eight Proven Parenting Principles for Raising Connected and Compassionate Children* Cofounder, *Attachment Parenting International*

The Science of
Mother-Infant Sleep

Current Findings on Bedsharing, Breastfeeding, Sleep Training, and Normal Infant Sleep

Edited by

Wendy Middlemiss, Ph.D.

&

Kathleen Kendall-Tackett, Ph.D., IBCLC, FAPA

Praeclarus Press, LLC

©2014 Wendy Middlemiss & Kathleen Kendall-Tackett.

www.PraeclarusPress.com

Praeclarus Press, LLC
2504 Sweetgum Lane
Amarillo, Texas 79124 USA
806-367-9950

www.PraeclarusPress.com

DISCLAIMER

The information contained in this publication is advisory only
and is not intended to replace sound clinical judgment or in-
dividualized patient care. The author disclaims all warranties,
whether expressed or implied, including any warranty as the
quality, accuracy, safety, or suitability of this information for
any particular purpose.

ISBN: 9781939807045

Cover Design: Ken Tackett

Acquisition & Development: Kathleen Kendall-Tackett

Copy Editing: Judy Torgus

Layout & Design: Ken Tackett & Kathleen Kendall-Tackett

Operations: Scott Sherwood

The Science of Mother-Infant Sleep

Foreword

Finding evidence-based information about infant nighttime care can be a daunting task for both parents and practitioners. Is bedsharing safe? When is it unsafe? What is the relationship between bedsharing and SIDS? Where does breastfeeding fit in? Is sleep training a good idea or is it harmful? What is normal infant and toddler sleep? These are the questions we set out to address.

A little over a year ago, we formed a small, international working group of practitioners and researchers who were experts in mother-infant sleep. We have worked to address some of the most prominent questions facing parents when it comes to infant sleep patterns, routines, and safety. It's been a productive year. We've written numerous blog posts, several white papers, and even produced a special issue of the journal *Clinical Lactation*. Our work is available online in a wide number of outlets. But it can be difficult to find.

In this volume, we bring together much of that work in one place. We wanted to provide a single resource so that this information can be easily located and is readily available. We hope that this collection of articles—addressing a diversity of concerns, and representing materials across different areas and disciplines—will become a resource for both parents and practitioners. Our goal is to help parents make decisions about infant sleep that are based on evidence, and to rest easy as they walk through the first year of their infants' lives.

Wendy Middlemiss
Kathleen Kendall-Tackett

Section I
Bedsharing, Breastfeeding, & SIDS

Chapter 1

"Don't Sleep with Big Knives"
Interesting (and Promising)
Developments in the
Mother-Infant Sleep Debate
Kathleen Kendall-Tackett

Figure 1: City of Milwaukee launches its latest anti-bedsharing campaign. The posters warn parents that bedsharing is as dangerous for babies as sleeping next to large butcher knives.

On November 9, 2011, amid much fanfare and media attention, the city of Milwaukee unveiled their latest campaign to promote safe infant sleep. The images are disturbing to say the least—they were designed that way.

"Co-sleeping deaths are the most preventable form of infant death in this community," Barrett said. "Is it shocking? Is it provocative?" asked Baker, the health commissioner. "Yes. But what is even more shocking and provocative is that 30 developed and underdeveloped countries have better (infant death) rates than Milwaukee."

A campaign such as this has a noble goal: to prevent infants from dying. But does this type of campaign keep infants safe? The tragic answer is "no." In less than two months after this campaign was launched, two more infants had died in Milwaukee in what the press described as "cosleeping deaths."

On January 3, 2012, WITI-TV, the affiliate Fox News in Milwaukee reported this:

One-Month-Old Infant Dies in Co-Sleeping Incident

Medical Examiner's Report Says Baby Was Sleeping On Floor with Three Other Children

> *The second death was of a 10-day-old infant who had died while sleeping with three other children on an adult bed.*

Neither of these infant sleep locations was safe and should not be classified as "bedsharing deaths." The sad take-away we can learn from these cases is that "simple messages," may be headline-grabbing.

But in the end, they do not communicate what parents need to know to keep their infants safe while sleeping.

In the same month as the Milwaukee campaign was launched, the American Academy of Pediatrics issued their new policy statement and follow-up technical report (American Academy of Pediatrics & Task Force on Sudden Infant Death Syndrome, 2011a, 2011b) on infant sleep-related deaths. In their press release, they stated that they were "expanding [the AAP guidelines] on safe sleep for babies, with additional information for parents on creating a safe environment for their babies to sleep."

When I first read through this statement, it didn't seem to differ all that much from previous statements, particularly on the issue many of us are interested in— namely, their recommendations regarding bedsharing. That recommendation did not really change. But in reading the full statement, there were some interesting, and dare I say hopeful, developments.

The AAP Policy Statement (2011a) lists their Levels A, B, and C recommendations. A-Level recommendations are those with the strongest evidence. Number 3 of their Level-A Recommendations is that parents and infants room share, but not bedshare (p. 1031). They based their recommendation on the results of a new meta-analysis of 11 studies comparing 2,404 cases where infants died (28.8% of whom bedshared) with 6,495 healthy controls (13.3% of whom bedshared). They calculated the odds ratio and found that it was 2.89 (95% CI, 1,99-4.18).

Based on their calculation, bedsharing increased the risk of SIDS by almost three times. But wait...The authors noted that there was "some heterogeneity in the analysis" (p. 45). The heterogeneity in question referred to the fact that *several of the studies included infant deaths that took place on a chair or couch* (a situation that greatly increases the risk of infant death), not just those that took place in an adult bed with a non-smoking, non-impaired parent.[1]

This issue has, of course, dogged the bedsharing debate for more than a decade. The authors themselves acknowledged that this was a difficulty (Vennemann et al., 2012).

> Only recent studies have disentangled infants sleeping with adults in a parental bed from infants sleeping with an adult on a sofa. This is certainly a limitation of the individual studies and hence of the meta-analysis (p. 47).

Hopeful sign number 1: the AAP statement specifically differentiates between bedsharing and the broader term, "cosleeping," which often includes all deaths that take place outside of a crib. I hope that this distinction will trickle down into future research studies.

And there's more. Vennemann et al. (2012) noted that bedsharing was much more hazardous with a smoking mother (OR=6.27; 95% CI, 3.94-9.99) than a non-smoking mother (OR=1.66; 95% CI, 0.91-3.01). So there was still some increased risk if an infant slept with a non-smoking mother. But remember that this analysis included studies where babies died on couches and chairs. The next analysis was by age of infant.

For infants <12 weeks, the odds ratio was 10.37

_____

1 An odds ratio of 1.0 indicates no increased risk. Above 1.0 means increased risk. The higher the number, the higher the risk.

(95% CI, 4.44-24.21). But for older infants, 1.02 (95% CI, 0.49-2.12), i.e., no increased risk. Another analysis looked at whether bedsharing was routine. They found that if bedsharing was routine, the odds ratio was 1.42 (95% CI, 0.85-2.38). If bedsharing was not routine, but happened on the last night, the odds ratio was 2.18 (95% CI, 1.45-2.38). The authors noted that the risk was NOT significantly elevated in the routine-bedsharing group (although I note that there does seem to be some elevation in risk, probably due to the studies that included couch sharing).

The next interesting issue is regarding their recommendations on chair or couch sharing with an infant. This has been a long-standing concern of mine due to the massively increased risk of infant death if parents fall asleep with infants on these surfaces. In fact, I have spoken with quite a few parents who routinely do this because they want to avoid bedsharing. Here's what AAP says.

> Because of the extremely high risk of SIDS and suffocation on couches and armchairs, infants *should not be fed* on a couch or armchair when there is a high risk that the parent might fall asleep (AAP, 2011a, p. 1033, emphasis added).

Further, they acknowledge—and seem to affirm—*feeding* babies in bed, but putting them in their own cribs for sleep.

> Therefore, if the infant is brought into the bed for feeding, comforting, and bonding, the infant should be returned to the crib when the parent is ready for sleep (AAP, 2011a, p. 1033).

Unfortunately, this statement does not acknowledge that it's quite easy to fall asleep in bed: 70% of mothers in our study who fed their babies in bed said that they fall asleep there (Kendall-Tackett, Cong, & Hale, 2010, this volume). And many a new parent would argue that that is precisely the point. There needs to be some recognition of, and planning for, that contingency. But other than that, I am happy to see this recommendation included.

The final point that I would like discuss is the role of breastfeeding in SIDS prevention, and how bedsharing has a role in sustaining breastfeeding. For example, Helen Ball (2007) found, in her longitudinal study of 97 initially breastfed infants, that breastfeeding for at least a month was significantly associated with regular bedsharing.

We, in the breastfeeding world, have been saying this for a very long time (Academy of Breastfeeding Medicine, 2008; McKenna & McDade, 2005; McKenna & Volpe, 2007). But now the *SIDS researchers* are saying it too. For example, Vennemann et al. (2009) found that breastfeeding reduced the risk of SIDS by 50%. (Yes, this is the same Vennemann whose meta-analysis was cited above.) Regarding breastfeeding, Vennemann et al. (2009) said the following.

> We recommend including the advice to breastfeed through six months of age in sudden infant death syndrome risk-reduction messages (p. e406).

Peter Blair and colleagues (Blair, Heron, & Fleming, 2010) went further and highlighted the role of bedsharing in maintaining breastfeeding. (Peter Blair is also a co-author on Vennemann et al., 2012.)

Advice on whether bedsharing should be discouraged needs to take into account the important relationship with breastfeeding (p. 1119).

So I am hopeful that we may be reaching a possible accord on this issue. While the AAP will probably never come straight out and recommend bedsharing, it would be helpful if they acknowledged that it will likely continue, and that our role is to help all parents sleep as safely as possible—either with or near their infants. Such a statement is possible. I'd like to close with the words from the Canadian Paediatric Society (Canadian Paediatric Society & Committee, 2004/2011).

Based on the available scientific evidence, the Canadian Paediatric Society recommends that for the first year of life, the safest place for babies to sleep is in their own crib, and in the parent's room for the first six months. However, the Canadian Paediatric Society also acknowledges that some parents will, nonetheless, choose to share a bed with their child...

The recommended practice of independent sleeping will likely continue to be the preferred sleeping arrangement for infants in Canada, but a significant proportion of families will still elect to sleep together...

The risk of suffocation and entrapment in adult beds or unsafe cribs will need to be addressed *for both practices* to achieve any reduction in this devastating adverse event (emphasis added).

References

Academy of Breastfeeding Medicine. (2008). ABM clinical protocol #6: Guideline on co-sleeping and breastfeeding. *Breastfeeding Medicine, 3*(1), 38-43.

American Academy of Pediatrics, & Task Force on Sudden Infant Death Syndrome. (2011a). Policy Statement: SIDS and other sleep-related deaths: Expansion of recommendations for a safe infant sleeping environment. *Pediatrics, 128*(5), 1030-1039.

American Academy of Pediatrics, & Task Force on Sudden Infant Death Syndrome. (2011b). Technical Report: SIDS and other sleep-related deaths: Expansion of recommendations for a safe infant sleeping environment. *Pediatrics, 128*(5), e1-e27.

Ball, H. L. (2007). Bed-sharing practices of initially breastfed infants in the first 6 months of life. *Infant & Child Development, 16*, 387-401.

Blair, P. S., Heron, J., & Fleming, P. J. (2010). Relationship between bed sharing and breastfeeding: Longitudinal, population-based analysis. *Pediatrics, 126*(5), e1119-e1126.

Canadian Paediatric Society, & Committee, C. P. (2004/2011). Recommendations for safe sleeping environments for infants and children. Retrieved from: http://www.cps.ca/english/statements/cp/cp04-02.htm#Recommendations

Kendall-Tackett, K. A., Cong, Z., & Hale, T. W. (2010). Mother-infant sleep locations and nighttime feeding behavior: U.S. data from the Survey of Mothers' Sleep and Fatigue. *Clinical Lactation, 1*(1), 27-30.

McKenna, J. J., & McDade, T. W. (2005). Why babies should never sleep alone: A review of the co-sleeping controversy in relation to SIDS, bedsharing, and breastfeeding. *Paediatric Respiratory Reviews, 6,* 134-152.

McKenna, J. J., & Volpe, L. E. (2007). Sleeping with baby: An internet-based sampling of parental experiences, choices, perceptions, and interpretations in a Western Industrialized context. *Infant & Child Development, 16,* 359-386.

Vennemann, M. M., Bajanowski, T., Brinkmann, B., Jorch, G., Yucesan, K., Sauerland, C.,...the GeSID Study Group. (2009). Does breastfeeding reduce the risk of sudden infant death syndrome. *Pediatrics, 123,* e406-e410.

Vennemann, M. M., Hense, H.-W., Bajanowski, T., Blair, P. S., Complojer, C., Moon, R. Y., & Kiechl-Kohlendorfer, U. (2012). Bedsharing and the risk of sudden infant death syndrome: Can we resolve the debate? *Journal of Pediatrics, 160,* 44-48.

Reprinted from *Clinical Lactation,* 2012, Vol. 3(1), 9-11. Used with permission.

Chapter 2

Sleeping with the Baby
Summary of Current Research Findings

Helen Ball

Who Sleeps with Their Baby and Why?

More babies bedshare in the first few weeks of life than at any other age. On any given night between 20% and 25% of babies under three months of age spend some time sharing a bed with a parent, and during their first three months up to 70% of babies in Euro-American households will have bedshared once or more (Ball, 2009; Blair & Ball, 2004; McCoy, Hunt, Lesko, Vezina, Corwin, Willinger, Hoffman, H.J., & Mitchell, 2004). When parents are interviewed about sleeping with their baby they give various reasons for doing so (Ateah & Hamelin, 2008; Ball, 2003; Culver, 2009).

Their answers express deeply rooted cultural or religious beliefs and parenting philosophies, invoke the physiological links between lactation and nighttime breastfeeding, and reflect the biological compulsion that drives bonding and the urge for close contact. On a practical level they also explain that sleeping with the baby makes nighttime care easier, helps them to monitor the baby, provide comfort, and yet obtain sleep.

Other parents report having nowhere else to put their baby at night, or that they have fallen asleep with their baby unintentionally. For breastfeeding mothers all of these reasons may apply, and so it is unsurprising that the largest group of bedsharers, around the globe, are breastfeeding mothers. Although it is a well-established fact that the majority of breastfeeding mothers sleep with their babies, the frequency and patterning with which they do so varies. Some do it all night, every night; some for part of the night; some only occasionally; and some accidentally fall asleep while feeding without ever meaning to.

Although many breastfeeding mothers report having been told that bedsharing is "wrong," almost every breastfeeding mother sometimes falls asleep with her baby, in bed or in a chair, or on a couch, regardless of whether or not she considers herself to be a "bedsharer." The "wrongness" of bedsharing may refer to a caution that it is unsafe—bearing the implication that to bedshare is irresponsible—or "wrong" may express a value judgment that parent-infant bedsharing is morally or culturally inappropriate.

However expressed or interpreted, the labeling of bedsharing as "wrong" is intended to invoke fear or guilt in the parent. It is vital, therefore, that all health professionals who support breastfeeding mothers are well informed about the issues surrounding sleep-sharing, and can help new mothers to make sense of how the research evidence relates to their own situations.

24

Questions, Questions, Questions...

Of course, many questions surround parent-infant sleep-sharing (be it in an adult bed, or sleeping together elsewhere). Does it "cause" SIDS (cot death)? Does it protect babies from SIDS? Do babies get smothered or overlain? Do mothers get more sleep, or less sleep? Is it dangerous to sleep with your baby if you don't breastfeed? What about babies who are very young, or premature, or very small? What if the parents smoke or drink? Does sleep-sharing help mothers to breastfeed? Does breastfeeding protect babies from sleepsharing risks? Where should you feed at night? Is it better to feed sitting up at night or lying down? How do you bedshare? Can you make the bed safe?

The issues surrounding bedsharing are not simple, and so many of the questions posed do not have simple answers. The research evidence is contradictory, and so is the guidance issued by different organizations. Most of the questions are also not easy to research, because bedsharing is difficult to disentangle from many other aspects of parenting that contribute to various outcomes, and very little research into bedsharing risks considers breastfed and non-breastfed infants separately.

What we know, therefore, is incomplete, and guidance comes with a certain "spin" that reflects the remit or priorities of the organization providing the guidance (Ball & Volpe, 2012) Parents therefore have to use their judgment in determining what works, or is "best," or is "safest," for them and their baby–and they need information in order to do so.

Over the past year, my colleague, Dr. Charlotte Russell, and I have been working with several organizations in the UK (La Leche League, National

25

Childbirth Trust, UNICEF Baby-Friendly Initiative)
to produce an Infant Sleep Information website (ISIS)
that aims to inform parents and health care providers
about the research evidence available on where and how
babies sleep (www.isisonline.org.uk). This editorial will
summarize some of the issues we discuss on the site, and
consider how the latest research is informing parents and
healthcare providers.

Why is Bedsharing Considered Dangerous?

There is a long history to the discussion of infant
sleep and safety that begins in our evolutionary past.
When I talk to public audiences, I often explain the
evolutionary characteristics of human infants and why
human mothers and infants require close physical contact
with one another in the first few months of life. Because
human babies are not completely developed at birth, they
need to be closely protected for several weeks, need to be
fed often, including at night.

My intention is to explain why mothers often
feel a need to sleep with their babies, and why babies
respond positively to close contact. Although this sleep
contact is a part of our evolved biology, it does not mean
it is without risk. I sometimes see biological explanations
used as an argument to dismiss safety concerns (e.g.,
"other mammals sleep with their babies without hurting
them").

While it is absolutely the norm among mammals
for mothers and their offspring to sleep in close contact,
we should remember that it is also common in nature
for mammals to die in infancy. Likewise infant mortality
has occurred at a high rate throughout human history
and babies have died while sleeping with their mothers,

for reasons that could be accidental, deliberate, or unrelated to where the baby slept. One aspect of infant mortality that came under early scrutiny was death due to overlying, which in the European Middle Ages was considered to be covert infanticide (Spinelli, 2003), and then in 19th century Scotland was linked to maternal alcohol consumption (Russell-Jones, 1985). To eliminate deliberate or accidental overlying deaths, the *Arcuccio* was invented in Italy to protect infants from their sleeping mothers (National Library of Medicine, 1895) (Figure 1).

Figure 1

The *Arcuccio*

> *An apparatus to prevent the overlying of infants.* British Medical Journal, *August 10, 1895. In other countries devices long used for infant carrying and daytime infant sleep (e.g. cradles and baskets) became co-opted as night-time infant sleep spaces as, with increasing prosperity, houses expanded and private bedrooms became fashionable. These influences have resulted in culturally-derived infant-sleep practices in many post-industrial nations that are now out of step with mother-infant evolved biology. This discordance between the recent cultural history, and the evolved history of infant care, is at the root of the bedsharing issue.*

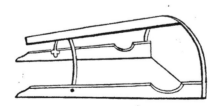

Source: National Library of Medicine. Used with permission.

As living standards and hygiene improved in prosperous countries during the 19th and 20th centuries, infant death rates declined to what are now their lowest points ever. One goal of Western medicine–to eliminate all preventable infant death–has been pursued extremely successfully in such settings, and as medical knowledge advanced, doctors with incubators and artificial feeding methods at their disposal could keep babies alive without a mother.

Eventually, mothers became superfluous to their infants' survival. By the mid-20th century Western infants predominantly slept in their own room, in specially designed furniture, and were fed chemically modified cow's milk formula. But although the presumed dangers of mothers' sleeping bodies were now absent, inexplicably, babies still died in their cribs, a phenomenon that became colloquially known as cot or crib death. Today Child Death Review Panels, Infant Mortality Boards, and Safeguarding Committees are prominent in many countries, and stringently examine every infant and child death in pursuit of future prevention.

Introducing SIDS...

From 1965 the unexpected death of an infant for which no cause could be found at post-mortem was classified as Sudden Infant Death Syndrome (SIDS), with a new code incorporated into the International Classification of Disease. SIDS, therefore, is not a cause from which babies die, but a category to which they are assigned if no cause can be found for their death. The search for the mechanisms underlying these deaths has so far been unsuccessful; it is still not known why babies die unexpectedly in their sleep. However, certain circumstances have been found to be associated with

SIDS, such as prone sleep position, exposure to smoking, and lack of breastfeeding.

These circumstances are commonly known as risk factors, and when multiple risk factors affect a single infant the risk of SIDS dramatically increases. Some risk factors are associated with intrinsic infant vulnerability, such as premature birth, low birthweight, or prenatal smoke exposure. Once a baby has been born, these factors cannot be altered. However, other factors are related to the environment of infant care, and are thought to provide a stressor that a vulnerable baby experiencing a critical period of development may be unable to overcome, the so-called "triple-risk SIDS model" (Filiano & Kinney, 1994).

Figure 2: The Triple-Risk Model of SIDS

These aspects of infant care are generally considered to be "modifiable" risks (e.g., sleep position, overwrapping, head-covering, feeding, pacifier use, parental smoking), and form the basis of many national SIDS prevention campaigns. A large measure of success has been achieved with some simple campaigns (such as "Back to Sleep"), but such "magic bullets" are rare and may actually now be hindering further SIDS-reduction efforts (Ball & Volpe, 2012).

...And Bedsharing

In 1986, anthropologist James McKenna hypothesized that one explanation for SIDS may involve the separation of babies from their mothers at night, a feature of infant care in certain Western countries that is historically and cross-culturally unique (McKenna, 1986). SIDS research at the time implicated suppressed infant arousals and breathing pauses (central apnea) as potential precursors to unexpected infant deaths, and McKenna proposed that infants sleeping in the sensory-rich environment of close sleep contact may be protected from apneic pauses and lack of arousal by maternal sounds, movements, and breathing (McKenna, Mosko, Dungy, & McAninch, 1990).

This was a popular hypothesis that many parents embraced, particularly those who already valued sleep contact with babies for the philosophical or practical reasons mentioned above. Although McKenna's research demonstrated the existence of a high degree of physiological synchrony between sleeping mothers and babies (McKenna, Ball, & Gettler, 2007), research on shared sleep environments indicated that bedsharing was another factor associated with increasing rather than decreasing risk of SIDS, and that the combination of bedsharing with a parent who smokes was particularly implicated (Blair, Fleming, Smith, Mitchell & Scragg, 1993).

For the past 20 years, discussion and studies regarding the real and presumed risks and benefits of bed-sharing have been on-going. No epidemiological studies have produced evidence that bedsharing definitely reduces SIDS risk, although there is strong evidence that co-sleeping (baby room-sharing with parent(s) for sleep) is protective. It is also now clear that certain behaviors and environments interact to make some forms of adult-infant sleep-sharing particularly hazardous (Blair, Fleming, Smith, Platt, Young, Nadin, Berry, & Golding, 1999; Mitchell & Scragg, 1993).

What Are the Risks?

Studies on the association between bedsharing and SIDS have been contradictory, with some finding evidence of an increased risk between bedsharing and SIDS only for the infants of smokers, and others finding the same association for non-smokers also. This has led to some countries and organizations advising parents to never bedshare, and others to avoid bedsharing under certain circumstances. The research evidence was recently reviewed in a meta-analysis that examined the data from 11 national case-control studies with data on SIDS and sleep location conducted between 1987 and 2006 (Vennemann, Hense, Bajanowski, Blair, Complojer, Moon, & Kiechl-Kohlendorfer, 2012).

Three studies were from the U.S., four from the UK, one each from Germany, Ireland, New Zealand and Norway. The review used a broad definition of bedsharing that encompassed the sharing of any sleep surface between adults and young children. Overall, the risk for SIDS increased almost three times for bedsharing in any sleep surface. Maternal smoking data were only available from four studies producing a six-fold increase in risk for maternal smoking and bedsharing (any sleep surface), compared to a 1.66 increase for non-smoking mothers, indicating a significantly increased risk only for smokers. Data on infant age and bedsharing (any sleep surface) were available from just three studies and were examined for all cases, regardless of smoking status.

31

The risk for infants less than 12 weeks old was about 10 times higher than for infants 12 weeks and older. However, without a further breakdown by smoking status, and no information on the type of sleep surface (e.g., bed vs. sofa), this apparent increased risk for younger infants is difficult to contextualize. It should also be remembered that the 12-week age-bracket is an arbitrary cut-off point and the definition of a "young infant" varies from study to study. In two studies routine bedsharing (any sleep surface) was not associated with SIDS, but five studies revealed a SIDS increase of over two-fold when sleep-sharing was not part of routine practice. Although described as a meta-analysis of 11 studies, only the overall risk of SIDS in relation to "bedsharing" actually incorporates data from the full-range of studies examined.

Where subgroup analyses were undertaken, these involved data from fewer than half the studies at best, and variables were examined in isolation from one another. It is frustrating to not have clear information on whether smoking status, or non-routine sleep-sharing, presents a disproportionately greater risk for young infants or what the contribution of sofa-sharing or alcohol consumption might be in this apparently vulnerable age group.

While this recent meta-analysis predominantly reviewed data that are now fairly old (including data from before and during the Back-to-Sleep campaigns, and the dramatic fall in SIDS deaths during the 1990s), more recent studies provide further insights. Where SIDS prevention guidance has emphasized cot/crib safety (supine sleep, avoidance of head covering and over-wrapping, removal of duvets, soft toys and bumpers, etc.) the rate of SIDS occurring in cots has fallen. Researchers are now beginning to apply the same principles to identifying factors involved in bedsharing safety.

Sleep location was examined in England by SWISS (South West Infant Sleep Study), a four-year population-based case-control study that compared 80 infant deaths meeting the criteria for SIDS with data from two age-matched control groups. The term "cosleeping" was used to define any sleep-sharing between an adult and baby on a bed or a sofa (Blair, Sidebotham, Evason-Coombe, Edmonds, Heckstall-Smith, & Fleming, 2009).

Among the SIDS infants, 54% died while co-sleeping compared with 20% who shared the reference sleep in both control groups. A significant interaction was found for infant deaths between co-sleeping and recent parental use of alcohol or drugs (31% vs. 3% random controls), and co-sleeping on a sofa (17% vs. 1%). The authors concluded that many of the SIDS infants had slept with an adult in a hazardous environment. The major influences on risk, regardless of markers for socioeconomic deprivation, were the use of alcohol or drugs before sharing a bed, and sofa-sharing.

Although data on whether or not mothers "attempted to breastfeed" were compared for cases and controls, no association was found with SIDS. However, more specific data on infant feeding type at time of death or reference sleep were not reported. It is now clear which characteristics of the shared sleep environment increase the risk of SIDS–smoking, alcohol and drug use, and sleeping with a baby on a sofa–and often these occur in combination. A study of bedsharing infant deaths in Alaska, for instance, found that in 99% of cases, at least one risk factor was present (e.g., maternal tobacco use; sleeping with a person impaired by consumption of some substance affecting awareness or arousal), and concluded that bedsharing alone does not increase the risk of infant deaths (Blabey & Gessner, 2009).

What about Accidental Infant Deaths, Such as Suffocation and Overlying?

In addition to SIDS that may occur during bedsharing, there is a growing literature on sleep location and accidental sudden unexpected death in infancy (SUDI). Distinguishing between SIDS and accidental SUDI has always been difficult due to the absence of clear diagnostic criteria for separating SIDS and soft suffocation. Where evidence for potential suffocation is circumstantial (e.g., presence of a sleep-partner), coroners may designate an infant death as "unascertained." Shared sleep environments have been implicated in infant suffocation deaths in recent UK and U.S. studies (Schnitzer, Covington, & Dykstra, 2012; Weber, Risdon, Ashworth, Malone, & Sebire, 2012).

Therefore, in addition to the issue of whether bedsharing carries an increased SIDS-risk in a given context, all parents should be alert to the possibility of accidental infant deaths when sleep-sharing. Parental responsibility is an important issue for both SIDS and accidental SUDI. If parents have considered safety issues related to bedsharing in advance of sleeping with their baby for the first time, the risks of accidentally falling asleep with the baby in a hazardous environment can be modulated. This is particularly important when alcohol and/or other drugs temporarily impair parental judgment, since it is a sober adult that should be making the decision about a baby's safety.

Breastfeeding and Bedsharing: What Do We Know?

Research confirms what breastfeeding mothers often report: that bedsharing facilitates frequent nighttime breastfeeding. Various studies have found that although bed-sharing breastfeeding mothers wake frequently to feed, they also wake for shorter periods, fall back to sleep more rapidly (Mosko, Richard, & McKenna, 1997), and achieve greater sleep duration (Quillan & Glenn, 2004), when compared to not bedsharing.

Recently a Swedish study reported an association between bedsharing and three or more nighttime wakings, but interpreted this as an association with sleep problems rather than as the need of breastfed infants to feed frequently, including at night (Mollborg, Wennergren, Norvenius, & Alm, 2011). Although the same authors reported an association in Sweden between bedsharing and being a single parent, in the UK we found the opposite association, with fewer single mothers bedsharing than those who were cohabiting (Ball, Moya, Fairley, Westman, Oddie, & Wright, 2012). Other studies have determined that breastfeeding is associated with greater or equivalent sleep duration than formula feeding in general, but have not examined sleep location (Doan, Gardiner, Gay, & Lee, 2007; Montgomery-Down, Clawges, & Santy, 2010).

The close interaction between breastfeeding and bedsharing has now been documented in 20 or more studies. Of particular interest is the observed association between bedsharing and greater duration of breastfeeding. In Brazil, for instance, researchers investigated breastfeeding outcomes at 12 months by interviewing mothers of 4,231 infants at birth, three and 12 months about their breastfeeding and bedsharing characteristics (Santos, Mota, Matijasevich, Barros, & Barros, 2009). Bedsharing was defined as habitual sharing of a bed between mother and child for all or part of the night. Breastfeeding prevalence at 12 months was 59% for those who bedshared at three months, and 44% for those who did not.

Among infants exclusively breastfed at three months, 75% of bedsharers were still breastfed at 12 months, versus 52% of non-sharers. The authors accepted these results as evidence that bedsharing protected against early weaning. However, the association tells us nothing about the direction of causality. The relationship may simply be that mothers who are inclined to breastfeed for longer may also be more inclined to bedshare.

Several years ago, we found a significant difference in breastfeeding frequency and infant sleep location when we conducted a randomized video study on the first two nights following birth in a hospital postpartum unit (Ball, Ward-Platt, Heslop, Leech, & Brown, 2006). Babies who shared their mothers' bed, or slept in a side-car crib attached to the bed, fed more than twice as frequently as babies who slept in a standard bassinette by the mothers' bed.

Video footage indicated that when babies woke during the night and began rooting for the breast, mothers in close proximity were alert to their feeding cues, and responded promptly. However, mothers whose babies were in a bassinette at their bedside did not feel their infants' movements or respond to their cues. These babies therefore missed many opportunities to initiate and practice latching and suckling, while the mothers did not receive the frequent nipple stimulation and prolactin surges that trigger prompt and copious milk production.

In a subsequent trial, we hypothesized that as sleep contact between mother and baby had been found to increase breastfeeding frequency, and because frequent breastfeeding is known to promote effective lactation, mothers and babies who were encouraged to sleep in close proximity following delivery may experience a longer duration of breastfeeding than those who slept apart, but in the same room (Ball, Ward-Platt, Howel, & Russell, 2011). In this trial, we randomized mothers and newborn infants to two different sleep conditions during their postpartum hospital stay: 1,204 pregnant women with an intention to breastfeed were recruited at a large UK hospital. Half were randomly allocated to normal rooming-in (stand-alone cot at bedside); the other half were allocated to close-contact (side-car crib clamped to the mother's bed-frame).

Following hospital discharge mothers reported weekly on their breastfeeding status and infant at-home sleep location; 870 mothers provided data for up to six months. Adjusting for maternal age, education, delivery type, and previous breastfeeding, we found no significant difference between the groups for duration of any or exclusive breastfeeding. Although we did not find that postnatal sleep proximity affected long-term breastfeeding outcomes in a busy tertiary hospital setting, the follow-up data reinforced the findings of previous studies.

Bedsharing at home was common (reported by 67% of side-car recipients vs. 64% of those rooming-in during postnatal stay), and those who bedshared in the first 13 weeks were twice as likely as non-sharers to breastfeed to six months (unpublished data). The short duration of current UK postpartum hospitalization means the directionality of the association now needs examining in the home, but how to randomize mothers and infants to different sleep locations (and ensure compliance) in a domestic setting is a methodological problem still to be solved!

Overall, to date we know that when new breastfeeding mothers bedshare they are more aware of and responsive to their infants' feeding cues, which assists with breastfeeding initiation. In the weeks and months following birth, breastfeeding mothers commonly bed-share to make nighttime feeding easier to manage, and those who bedshare sleep more and breastfeed for longer than those who sleep apart. This may be an important suggestion for working mothers who continue to breastfeed once they return to work, or decide to stop breastfeeding because they are soon returning to work. Even if they wake more often during the night to breastfeed their infants, in general they sleep as many hours or more than non-cosleepers (an advantage for themselves), and they continue to breastfeed for an overall longer period (an advantage for their baby).

Now we must consider the degree to which the benefits of bedsharing for breastfeeding mothers and babies are offset by real or presumed risks.

Breastfeeding, Bedsharing, and Risks

Breastfed babies are sometimes the victims of SIDS, although SIDS deaths are less frequent among babies who are breastfed than those who are not. A meta-analysis of breastfeeding and SIDS confirmed that breastfed babies had less than half the risk of SIDS than those who were not breastfed, and that the effect was stronger when breastfeeding was exclusive (Hauck, Thompson, Tanabe, Moon, & Vennemann, 2011). However, no SIDS case-control studies have
38

determined the SIDS risk of bedsharing in an adult bed by currently breastfeeding infants in the absence of the well-established risks (smoking, alcohol use and drug consumption), with the exception of a study in the Netherlands whose results are considered inconclusive because of the small sample, the lack of breakdown by breastfeeding status, and the lack of data on other risk factors (Ruys, de Jonge, Brand, Engelberts, & Semmekrot, 2007). For all these reasons, this study was excluded from the above meta-analysis.

Other researchers have produced estimates in attempts to address the same issue. Carpenter used data from 20 regions in Europe to estimate that the SIDS-rate for breastfed, bedsharing infants would be twice that of breastfed non-bedsharing infants, reflecting an increase from 1 to 2 per 10,000 in the cumulative number of deaths estimated by six months of age (Carpenter, Irgen, Blair, England, Fleming, Huber, Jorch, & Schreuder, 2004). The same estimates for non-breastfed infants produced rates of 4/10,000 and 11/10,000 for not bedsharing and bedsharing respectively.

Compared to the UK national SIDS-rate of 1/2,000, both the estimates for breastfed infants, either in or out of the bedsharing environment, are therefore very low, and an excess risk for non-breastfed babies who bedshare is indicated. In an examination of the patterns of bedsharing and breastfeeding over time between birth and 45 months of age for 14,000 families from the ALSPAC (Avon Longitudinal Study of Parents and Children) cohort study (infants born in 1991 and 1992), latent-class analysis (a powerful multivariate statistical method that identifies unobservable subgroups within a population) was used to identify groups of families based on their bedsharing characteristics (Blair, Heron, & Fleming, 2010).

The authors concluded that families most likely to bedshare in the months following birth were also those most likely to breastfeed, and that the characteristics of these families placed them at very low risk of SIDS. Any benefit from preventing bedsharing in this group, therefore, would be very small, and by following such advice, breastfeeding would probably suffer. The authors recommend that risk-reduction messages to prevent SIDS be targeted specifically to unsafe infant care practices; in this way infant mortality prevention would avoid undermining breastfeeding outcomes for those infants already at low risk of unexpected death.

Balancing Information

The challenge of balancing the public health benefits of exclusive breastfeeding to six months of age with the safeguarding/infant mortality agenda of preventing all infant deaths will require creative solutions. Breastfeeding cannot protect an infant from risks introduced by hazardous parental behavior, and so guidance that infants are safest sleeping in a crib next to their parents' bed is defensible as a general public health message; but this message must also acknowledge that not all parent-infant bedsharing is inherently dangerous, and that breastfeeding, bedsharing mothers and infants are a particularly low-risk group.

It is, therefore, not defensible to advise, or imply, that bedsharing is lethal and should never be practiced under any circumstances. To do so is also alienating. Recent data from the U.S., where fear-tactics have been implemented in anti-bedsharing campaigns, indicate that simple messages designed to demonize bedsharing are rejected by the parents at whom they are targeted (Ball & Volpe, 2012). In Milwaukee, the infamous butcher's knife and tombstone messages posted on billboards (see Chapters 1 and 3, this volume) have failed to produce a sustained reduction in infant mortality in the highest-risk groups.

Cultural infant-care traditions, and personal parenting beliefs that incorporate bedsharing as a valued component of parenting, will not respond to campaigns that treat sleep contact as a modifiable risk factor or simple infant-care practice (such as sleep position). In a recent publication, I argue that much bedsharing research has so far failed to recognize the importance of infant sleep location to ethnic and sub-cultural identity (Ball & Volpe, 2012). We include breastfeeding mothers as a particular subcultural group who reject many of the dominant ideologies regarding infant care, particularly mother-infant separation, and we call for more sensitive and targeted information alongside the continued pursuit of detailed research that helps in the development of more nuanced guidance regarding bedsharing. This is the kind of information we aim to make available on the ISIS website. Please let us know how we're doing (www. isisonline.org.uk).

References

Ateah, C.A., & Hamelin, K.J. (2008). Maternal bedsharing practices, experiences, and awareness of risks. *Journal of Obstetric, Gynecologic, & Neonatal Nursing, 37,* 274-281.

Ball, H. (2009) Airway covering during bed-sharing. *Child Care, Health & Development, 35,* 728-737.

Ball, H.L. (2003). Breastfeeding, bed-sharing, and infant sleep. *Birth, 30,* 181-188.

Ball, H.L., Moya, E., Fairley, L., Westman, J., Oddie, S., & Wright, J. (2012). Bed- and sofa-sharing practices in a UK bi-ethnic population. *Pediatrics, 129,* e673-e681.

Ball, H.L., & Volpe, L.E. (2012). Sudden Infant Death Syndrome (SIDS) risk reduction and infant sleep location--Moving the discussion forward. *Social Science & Medicine;* doi:10.1016/j. socscimed.2012.03.025.

Ball, H.L., Ward-Platt, M.P., Heslop, E., Leech, S.J., & Brown, K.A. (2006). Randomized trial of infant sleep location on the postnatal ward. *Archives of Diseases of Childhood, 91,* 1005-1010.

Ball, H.L., Ward-Platt, M.P., Howel, D., & Russell, C. (2011). Randomized trial of sidecar crib use on breastfeeding duration (NECOT). *Archives of Diseases of Childhood, 96,* 630-634.

Blabey, M.H., & Gessner, B.D. (2009). Infant bed-sharing practices and associated risk factors among births and infant deaths in Alaska. *Public Health Rep, 124,* 527-534.

Blair, P.S., & Ball, H.L. (2004). The prevalence and characteristics associated with parent-infant bed-sharing in England. *Archives of Diseases of Childhood, 89,* 1106-1110.

Blair, P.S., Fleming, P.J., Smith, I.J., Platt, M.W., Young, J., Nadin, P., Berry, P.J., & Golding, J. (1999). Babies sleeping with parents: case-control study of factors influencing the risk of sudden infant death syndrome. CESDI SUDI research group. *British Medical Journal, 319,* 1457-1461.

Blair, P.S., Heron, J., & Fleming, P.J. (2010). Relationship between bed sharing and breastfeeding: longitudinal, population-based analysis. *Pediatrics, 126,* e1119-e1126.

Blair, P.S., Sidebotham, P., Evason-Coombe, C., Edmonds, M., Heckstall-Smith, E.M., & Fleming P. (2009). Hazardous cosleeping environments and risk factors amenable to change: case-control study of SIDS in south west England. *British Medical Journal, 339,* b3666.

Carpenter, R.G., Irgens, L.M., Blair, P.S., England, P.D., Fleming, P., Huber, J., Jorch, G., & Schreuder, P. (2004). Sudden unexplained infant death in 20 regions in Europe: Case control study. *Lancet, 363,* 185-191.

Culver, E.D. (2009). Exploring bed-sharing mothers' motives and decision-making for getting through the night intact: A grounded theory. *Journal of Midwifery and Women's Health.* American College of Nurse-Midwives, Silver Spring MD.

Doan, T., Gardiner, A., Gay, C.L., & Lee, K.A. (2007). Breast-feeding increases sleep duration of new parents. *Journal of Perinatal & Neonatal Nursing, 21,* 200-206.

Filiano, J.J., & Kinney, H.C. (1994). A perspective on neuropathologic findings in victims of the sudden infant death syndrome: The triple-risk model. *Biology of the Neonate, 65,* 194-197.

Hauck, F.R., Thompson, J.M., Tanabe, K.O., Moon, R.Y., & Vennemann, M.M. (2011). Breastfeeding and reduced risk of sudden infant death syndrome: A meta-analysis. *Pediatrics, 128,* 103-110.

McCoy, R.C., Hunt, C.E., Lesko, S.M., Vezina, R., Corwin, M.J., Willinger, M., Hoffman, H.J., & Mitchell, A.A. Frequency of bed sharing and its relationship to breastfeeding. (2004). *Journal of Developmental & Behavioral Pediatrics, 25,* 141-149.

McKenna, J.J. (1986). An anthropological perspective on the sudden infant death syndrome (SIDS): The role of parental breathing cues and speech breathing adaptations. *Medical Anthropology, 10,* 992.

McKenna, J.J., Ball, H.L., & Gettler, L.T. (2007). Mother-infant cosleeping, breastfeeding and sudden infant death syndrome: What biological anthropology has discovered about normal infant sleep and pediatric sleep medicine. *American Journal of Physical Anthropology, Suppl. 45,* 133-161.

McKenna, J.J., Mosko, S., Dungy, C., & McAninch, J. (1990). Sleep and arousal patterns of co-sleeping human mother/infant pairs: A preliminary physiological study with implications for the study of sudden infant death syndrome (SIDS). *American Journal of Physical Anthropology, 183,* 331-347.

Mitchell, E.A., & Scragg, R. (1993). Are infants sharing a bed with another person at increased risk of sudden infant death syndrome? *Sleep, 16,* 387-389.

Mollborg, P., Wennergren, G., Norvenius, S.G., & Alm B. (2011). Bed-sharing among six-month-old infants in western Sweden. *Acta Paediatrica, 100,* 226-230.

Montgomery-Downs, H.E., Clawges, H.M., & Santy, E.E. (2010). Infant feeding methods and maternal sleep and daytime functioning. *Pediatrics, 126,* e1562-e1568.

Mosko, S., Richard, C., & McKenna, J. (1997). Maternal sleep and arousals during bedsharing with infants. *Sleep, 20,* 142-150.

National Library of Medicine. (1895). *The Arcuccio.* Retrieved from: http://www.ncbi.nlm.nih.gov/pmc/articles/PMC2508215/pdf/brmedj08781-0040.pdf

Quillin, S.I., & Glenn, L.L. (2004). Interaction between feeding method and co-sleeping on maternal-newborn sleep. *Journal of Obstetric, Gynecologic, & Neonatal Nursing, 33,* 580-588.

Russell-Jones, D.L. (1985). Sudden infant death in history and literature. *Archives of Diseases of Childhood, 60,* 278-281.

Ruys, J.H., de Jonge, G.A., Brand, R., Engelberts, A.C., & Semmekrot, B.A. (2007). Bed-sharing in the first months of life: A risk factor for sudden infant death. *Acta Paediatrica, 96,* 1399-1403.

Schnitzer, P.G., Covington, T.M., & Dykstra, H.K. (2012). Sudden unexpected infant deaths: Sleep environment and circumstances. *American Journal of Public Health, 102,* 1204-1212.

Santos, I.S., Mota, D.M., Matijasevich, A., Barros, A.J., & Barros, F.C. (2009). Bed-sharing at 3 months and breast-feeding at 1 year in southern Brazil. *Journal of Pediatrics, 155,* 505-509.

Spinelli, M.G. (2003). *Infanticide: psychosocial and legal perspectives on mothers who kill.* Arlington, VA: American Psychiatric Publishing.

Vennemann, M.M., Hense, H.W., Bajanowski, T., Blair, P.S., Complojer, C., Moon, R.Y., & Kiechl-Kohlendorfer, U. (2012). Bed sharing and the risk of sudden infant death syndrome: can we resolve the debate? *Journal of Pediatrics, 160*, 44-48.

Weber, M.A., Risdon, R.A., Ashworth, M.T., Malone, M., & Sebire, N.J. (2012). Autopsy findings of co-sleeping-associated sudden unexpected deaths in infancy: relationship between pathological features and asphyxial mode of death. *Journal of Paediatrics & Child Health, 48*, 335-341.

Chapter 3

Mother–Infant Sleep Locations and Nighttime Feeding Behavior

U.S. Data from the Survey of Mothers' Sleep and Fatigue

Kathleen Kendall–Tackett
Zhen Cong
Thomas W. Hale

The controversy around mother–infant bedsharing continues to grow. In order to make sound policy recommendations, policy makers need current data on where infants sleep, and how families handle nighttime feedings. The present study is a survey of 4,789 mothers of infants 0–12 months of age in the U.S. The findings indicate that almost 60% of mothers bedshare and that this occurs throughout the first year. These findings also indicate that 25% of mothers are falling asleep with their infants in dangerous sleep locations, such as chairs, sofas, or recliners. Recommendations for promoting safe infant sleep are made.

In 2005, the American Academy of Pediatrics (AAP) Task Force on SIDS issued a statement on safe sleeping practices for infants, recommending that infants "should not bedshare during sleep" (p. 1252). [NOTE: While SUID (sudden unexplained infant death) may be a more accurate term, all of the studies cited used the term SIDS. We have chosen to use the term SIDS for consistency.]

Subsequent to the AAP Statement, some local municipalities have attempted to make this point more strongly by telling parents to never bedshare, with public-service advertising designed to shock parents into compliance (see Figure 1).

Figure 1: Public service warning to new parents about the dangers of bedsharing.

In an attempt to present a simple "single message" to parents, these campaigns have, unfortunately, mischaracterized research findings regarding SIDS and infant sleep by indicating that "safe" sleep occurs in a crib and "unsafe" sleep occurs anywhere else. But the SIDS studies themselves indicate risk factors for infant death are not quite so simple.

For example, a study of 325 SIDS cases from the UK found no excess risk of SIDS for term infants (>2,500 g at birth) who bedshared with non-smoking parents (Blair et al., 2006a). In a study of 238 SIDS cases in New Jersey, only 39% (N=93) were "bedsharing." Of these, only 21 were breastfeeding, and most of these had other SIDS risk factors, such as non-supine position; pillows or fluffy blankets in the sleep area; substance abuse; couch/recliner sharing; or maternal smoking (Ostfeld et al., 2006). In 78% of these cases, families had anywhere from two to seven risk factors (Ostfeld et al., 2010).

Confusion of Terminology in Defining Bedsharing

One problematic aspect of this debate is confusion of terminology, such as including sofa or recliner sharing in definitions of "bedsharing." These behaviors are not equivalent in terms of risk. For example, in a Scottish sample of 123 SIDS cases, the odds ratio of SIDS for couch/chair sharing was 66.9 (95% CI=2.8, 1597), compared to 1.07 for bedsharing infants 11 weeks or older (95% CI=0.32, 3.56). Of the 123 cases in this sample, 46 were bedsharing and 77 were not (Tappin et al., 2005).

As dangerous as sofa-sharing is, it appears to be on the rise. In a 20-year population-based study in the UK, Blair and colleagues (2006b) found that while the number of SIDS cases dropped substantially as a result of the Back-to-Sleep campaign, there was an increase in "cosleeping" deaths due to "an increase in the number of deaths in infants sleeping with their parents on a sofa" (p. 314). They strongly recommended that parents avoid this dangerous sleep environment.

Anti-Bedsharing Campaigns Launched in Response to Local Infants Death

Many anti-bedsharing campaigns are launched in response to local infant deaths. While understandable, policies formed under these circumstances can be problematic. For example, the rate of SIDS deaths in the U.S. is 0.56 per 1,000, or 0.0006% of infants. Of these, roughly 40% occur outside of cribs (0.00024%), including many unsafe sleep surfaces. It is not sound to make recommendations for all infants based on what happens to a very small percentage.

Where Do Babies Sleep?

So how are average parents handling babies' nighttime needs? Lahr and colleagues (2007), in a sample of 1,867 mothers from Oregon, found that 76% of mother bedshare at least some of the time. These findings were based on PRAMS data collected in 1998-1999, before the current controversy or policy recommendations. Policy makers need more current data on what parents are actually doing. How are mothers handling nighttime feedings? Are parents complying with "never bedshare" policies? Are there any groups of parents more or less likely to bedshare?

The present study was designed to answer these questions. We conducted a large online survey of mothers with infants ages 0-12 months, in an effort to answer several key questions with regard to infant sleep.

- Where are infants sleeping throughout the night?

- Are mothers sleeping with infants in unsafe settings, such as couches and recliners?

- What are mothers' reasons for using their sleep practices?

- Are mothers telling others, including health care providers, about where their infants sleep?

Methods

Study Participants

The data included in this analysis were from the U.S. mothers (N=4,789) who participated in the Survey of Mothers' Sleep and Fatigue in 2008-2009. The total sample from this study was 6,410, representing 59 countries. Although this sample was comprised primarily of breastfeeding mothers, they were evenly divided in their beliefs about where babies should sleep: 35% in the parent's bed, 34% in a crib in another room, and 31% in the parents' room.

Sample Recruitment

The sample was recruited via announcements and flyers distributed to WIC Breastfeeding Coordinators, U.S. State Breastfeeding Coalition Coordinators, U.S. Lactation Consultants, and La Leche League Leaders. The investigators described the study and asked for assistance in recruiting mothers. Flyers and cards were distributed electronically and via hard copy, with a Web link for the survey. This survey was open to all mothers with babies 0-12 months of age who had access to the Internet.

Survey Development

The research questions were taken from the 253-item Survey of Mothers' Sleep and Fatigue. The questions were predominately close-ended in format and were developed for this study via open-ended interviews with mothers and feedback from mothers and health care professionals.

Data Collection

Data were collected via an online survey that was available on the Texas Tech University Department of Pediatrics website. A screening question asked for the baby's age. If the response was 12 months or less, the mother was allowed to continue the survey. The survey and data collection procedure was reviewed and approved by the Texas Tech University School of Medicine Institutional Review Board.

Results & Discussion

Bedsharing Rates

The results of this survey suggest that bedsharing is common in the U.S., despite campaigns against it. The percentages of bedsharing families varied considerably depending on how the question was worded. When asked, "where does your baby sleep, that is, where does your baby spend most of the night?," 44% mothers indicated that their babies were in their beds (see Figure 2). When asked where their babies start the night, only 31% were bedsharing (see Figure 3). When asked where babies end the night, 59% of infants were bedsharing.

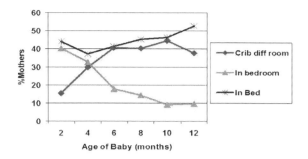

Figure 2: *Where does your baby sleep? That is, where does your baby spend most of the night?* **U.S. Sample (N=4,434), $\chi^2(10)=440.425$, p<.0001**

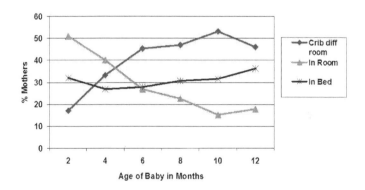

Figure 3: *Where does your baby start the night?* **U.S. Sample (N=4,336), $\chi^2(10)=415.023$, p<.00015**

Our findings indicate that bedsharing rates persist throughout the first year, and were as high as 62% (Figure 4). These figures also indicate that infant sleep locations are fluid and change over the course of the night.

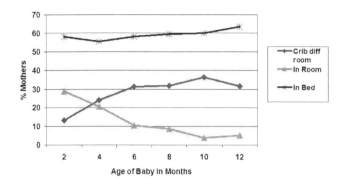

Figure 4: *Where does your baby end the night?* **U.S. Sample (N=4,399), $\chi^2(10)=365.36$, p<.0001**

Although bedsharing is common across demographic categories, it is significantly more common in single, divorced or separated women, and in African American, American Indian, and Caucasian women. Bedsharing was more common among lower–income families, but still occurred in slightly less than half of affluent families.

A similar pattern emerged based on education. While more educated mothers were slightly less likely to bedshare, over half of highly educated mothers still did so. Bedsharing was significantly more common when mothers were exclusively breastfeeding.

Location of Nighttime Feedings

Of mothers in our sample, approximately half (N=2,103) were still feeding their babies at night. Nighttime feedings took place either in bed (44%) or on a chair, recliner, or sofa (55%). When asked if they sometimes fall asleep in this location, not surprisingly, 72% of mothers who feed in bed indicated that they fall asleep. More alarming is that 44% of mothers feeding on chairs, sofas or recliners fall asleep there. This group comprises 25% of the group that is still feeding at night.

Women with higher levels of education and income were more likely to feed their babies at night on chairs, couches, or recliners (see Figures 5 & 6). High-income, highly educated mothers are generally "low risk" in terms of infant mortality. Possibly in an attempt to avoid bedsharing, this generally low-risk group is engaging in high–risk behavior.

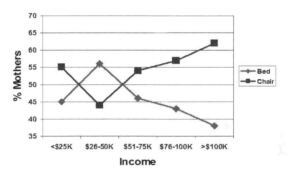

Figure 5: Night feeding location by household income, N=2,005 $\chi^2(4)$=29.558, p<.0001

What People Are Saying to Mothers

Bedsharing mothers (86%) were significantly more likely to receive negative feedback from friends and family about where their babies sleep than when babies roomshare (8%) or sleep in cribs in a different room (6%; $\chi^2(2)$=681.64, p<.0001). Further, bedsharing families (70%) are significantly less likely to tell their health care providers about where their babies end the night than those whose babies roomshare (13%) or whose babies sleep in different rooms (17%; $\chi^2(2)$=132.75, p<.0001).

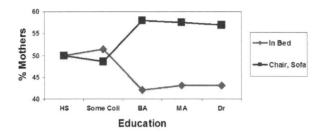

Figure 6: Maternal education by nighttime feeding location, N=2,104, $X^2(4)=12.47$, p<.014

These findings suggest that the mothers in our study are well aware of the prohibitions against bedsharing. So why do they persist?

Reasons Mothers Give for Their Sleep Arrangements

When asked about their reasons for their current sleep arrangements, bedsharing mothers were significantly more likely to indicate that it was the right way to do it (61%) than mothers who roomshare (13%,) or have babies in a different room (26%: $\chi^2(2)=6.90$, p<.032).

Bedsharing mothers were also more likely to indicate that their sleep arrangement was the only way that worked for them (69%) as compared to those who roomshare (9%) or have babies in a different room (22%: $\chi^2(2)=162.9$, p<.0001). In other words, bedsharing mothers have both ideological ("the right way to do it") and pragmatic ("the only way that worked") reasons for bedsharing that are unlikely to change due to pressure from health care providers or public-health initiatives.

These findings are similar to those of Chianese et al. (2009), who conducted a focus-group study with inner–city mothers. These mothers cited the following reasons for bedsharing: better mother-infant sleep, convenience, tradition, child safety, and parent-child emotional needs. They indicated that clinicians' advice did not influence their decisions. But they indicated that they would appreciate advice on safe bedsharing.

Conclusions

- Despite ongoing anti-bedsharing campaigns, U.S. parents continue to bedshare in high numbers.

- Bedsharing families cite both ideological and pragmatic reasons for sleeping with their babies. They appear well–aware of prohibitions against bedsharing, but consistent with the results of previous studies, the majority continue to bedshare.

- In a possible attempt to avoid bedsharing, 55% of mothers feed their babies at night on chairs, recliners or sofas. Forty-four percent (25% of the sample) admit that they fall asleep with their babies in these locations. Of all sleep locations, chairs, sofas and recliners are by far the most dangerous and dramatically increase the risk of suffocation.

Recommendations

Safe-sleep campaigns should include information on safe bedsharing. In absence of this information, parents are likely to continue bedsharing, but may do so in unsafe ways. Alternatively, safe-sleep campaigns could provide other strategies, such as encouraging babies to sleep on adjacent, yet separate, surfaces.

References

American Academy of Pediatrics, Task Force on Sudden Infant Death Syndrome. (2005). The changing concept of sudden infant death syndrome: Diagnostic coding shifts, controversies regarding the sleeping environment, and new variables to consider in reducing risk. *Pediatrics, 116*, 1245–1255.

Blair, P. S., Platt, M. W., Smith, I. J., Fleming, P. J., & Group, C. S. R. (2006a). Sudden infant death syndrome and sleeping position in pre–term and low birth weight infants: An opportunity for targeted intervention. *Archives of Disease of Childhood, 91*(2), 101–106.

Blair, P. S., Sidebotham, P., Berry, P. J., Evans, M., & Fleming, P. J. (2006b). Major epidemiological changes in sudden infant death syndrome: A 20–year population–based study. *Lancet, 367*, 314–319.

Chianese, J., Ploof, D., Trovato, C., & Chang, J. C. (2009). Inner–city caregivers' perspectives on bed sharing with their infants. *Academic Pediatrics, 9*(1), 26–32.

Lahr, M. B., Rosenberg, K. D., & Lapidus, J. A. (2007). Maternal–infant bedsharing: Risk factors for bedsharing in a population-based survey of new mothers and implications for SIDS risk reduction. *Maternal Child Health Journal, 11*, 277–286.

Ostfeld, B. M., Esposito, L., Perl, H., & Hegyi, T. (2010). Concurrent risks in sudden infant death syndrome. *Pediatrics, 125*, 447–453.

Ostfeld, B. M., Perl, H., Esposito, L., Hempstead, K., Hinnen, R., Sandler, A., et al. (2006). Sleep environment, positional, lifestyle, and demographic characteristics associated with bed sharing in sudden infant death syndrome: A population–based study. *Pediatrics, 118,* 2051–2059.

Tappin, D., Ecob, R., Stat, S., & Brooke, H. (2005). Bedsharing, roomsharing, and sudden infant death syndrome in Scotland: A case-control study. *Journal of Pediatrics, 147,* 32–37.

Reprinted from *Clinical Lactation,* 2010, Vol. 1(1), 27-31. Used with permission.

Chapter 4

SIDS: Risks and Realities
A Response to Recent Findings on Bedsharing and SIDS Risk

Sarah Ockwell-Smith
Wendy Middlemiss
Tracy Cassels
Helen Stevens
Darcia Narvaez

A recent meta-analysis by Carpenter et al. (2013) examined the risk factors for Sudden Infant Death Syndrome (SIDS). While we commend Carpenter et al. for examining risks associated with incidence of SIDS, we question their conclusions, and consider them unsubstantiated. Their analysis used faulty and missing data, and they did not account for confounding criteria used to define bedsharing and risks—a challenge in any meta-analysis.

Carpenter et al. examined some of the most salient risk factors for SIDS events—infant sleep position, parental cigarette smoking, infant birthweight, and age. These risks have been well-documented as increasing risk of SIDS events. Thus, it is not surprising or informative to note that these factors remain risks in a re-evaluation of these findings.

While the risks examined do contribute significantly to increasing possibility of SIDS (see Figure 1), so do other factors, such as bedding and temperature (see Box below for lists of risks not considered). Without consideration of these risks, it is not possible to determine that one variable, such as bedsharing itself, is *inherently* responsible for risk remaining in this study. Nor is it possible to say that one of the variables within the nighttime care routine, such as breastfeeding, is not protective.

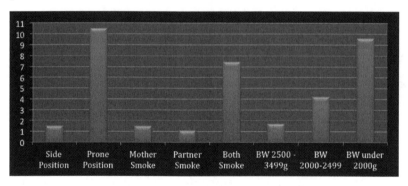

Figure 1: Adjusted Odds Ratios (AOR) from Carpenter et al. (2013) NOTE: *BW=Birthweight*

Major Limitations

In addition to these major limitations in making broad, sweeping statements about risk based on this meta-analysis, there are two additional issues that are of significant concern in the paper as a whole. We address these herein.

Treatment of Breastfeeding

The first is the treatment of breastfeeding. Buried deep in the last section of the paper is the recommendation that breastfeeding be supported as a mechanism for protecting infant health, the construction of the hypotheses explored here leads to a very different framework.

In attempting to examine whether breastfeeding protects against the risk of SIDS when parents bedshare, the authors seem to jumble the role of breastfeeding in a manner that undermines one of their stated objectives: to address health costs associated with early infant care by reducing SIDS events. Further, the authors seem to overlook the Adjusted Odds Ratio (AOR) for bottle-feeding and SIDS risk (see Figure 2).

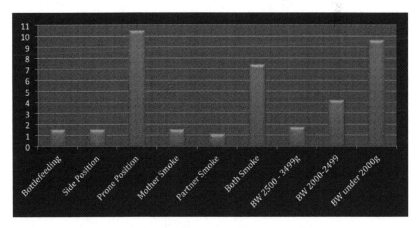

Figure 2: Adjusted Odds Ratios including bottlefeeding from Carpenter et al. (2013) NOTE: *BW = Birthweight*

In examining the role of breastfeeding, the authors seem to overlook one essential aspect of infant development—breastfeeding contributes positively to both immediate and later infant health outcomes, not just a reduction in SIDS, though it serves as a protective factor there as well (Alm et al., 2002; Ford et al., 1993; Horne et al., 2004; McVea et al., 2000; Mitchell et al., 1992; Mosko et al., 1997; Scragg et al., 1993).

Thus, important in consideration from any perspective is to encourage mothers' breastfeeding through the infant's first year of life. However, the authors seem to couch this protective factor in the arena of risk, thus confusing the message for practitioners and parents.

Instead of looking at how each of the variables in the dataset can contribute to risk of infants' breathing or compromise arousal—the authors focus on whether the act of breastfeeding **protects against all risk of SIDS**. Clearly that is a standard that cannot be reached. We can, however, easily answer whether breastfeeding protects against SIDS regardless of parental behavior without the necessity of meta-analyses, the imputing of data from 5 of 12 variables, the compromising operational definitions of nighttime-care contexts.

The answer is simple, though not informative. Yes, there is still a risk. Why? Because there are multiple risk factors that compromise infants' capacity to breathe and infants' ability to arouse. Breastfeeding does not vaccinate against all risks (e.g., a pillow in the face).

The authors give lip service to breastfeeding, but suggest that any claim that bedsharing helps breastfeeding is ill-advised. The use of the Netherlands as a key example of how lowering bedsharing, but increasing breastfeeding rates, fails to make their point given the relatively low rates and low increases over the 10-year period discussed (a rise of 7% and 8% of *any* breastfeeding at three and six months respectively).

It is unclear if the strong anti-bedsharing campaign inhibited greater growth in breastfeeding, something that should be of concern when examining the costs associated with infant health. In the U.S. alone, a cost-analysis found that if we could get 80% mothers to breastfeed exclusively for six months (the WHO recommendations), the U.S. would save $10.5 billion a year in health-related costs (Bartick & Reinhold, 2009).

Furthermore, it is misguided and dangerous to argue that if bedsharing were recognized as a means of supporting breastfeeding that we would see more SIDS events. Even more dangerous is to abandon support of breastfeeding in favor of supporting breastfeeding if it detoured bedsharing.

Although the AOR in the current meta-analysis suggests that bottle-feeding is a lower risk factor than bedsharing (the validity of which will be discussed below), it only concerns itself with SIDS events, not the more general protective benefits of breastfeeding on infant health.

As previously mentioned, breastfeeding confers many health benefits, both immediate and long-term, to children (Horta et al., 2007; Ip et al., 2007; Martin et al., 2005; Owen et al., 2002). To only consider SIDS events ignores the effects of lower breastfeeding rates on myriad other diseases.

Risk Factors Not Included in the Analysis

The second issue pertains to the risk factors included and not included in the analysis. The authors have thankfully confirmed some of the major risk factors associated with SIDS, both independently and when interacting with sleep location, such as sleep position, parent smoking, alcohol use, drug use, birthweight, and infant age.

The authors solidified many risks, as they were stated individually in the reports associated with each large data set. With this, researchers, practitioners, and parents now have a clear documentation of these specific risks.

They clearly confirmed the known risks and quantification of those risks. For example, maternal smoking remains to be one of the most salient risks associated with SIDS—with paternal smoking contributing to risk as well. Similarly, infant sleep position (i.e., prone and side sleep), contribute significant risk of SIDS events.

Missing from the analysis are other known risk factors that are recognized as part of the triple-risk model: critical developmental period (infant age), environmental context (bedding), or infant vulnerability (prematurity). Additionally, the authors fail to include data sets that do examine these risk factors and that come to very different conclusions about the inherent risk of bedsharing on SIDS events (e.g., Blabey & Gessner, 2009).

The authors argue that bedsharing is causally related to SIDS events via theories about infant breathing and arousability. Specifically, the authors state:

The proposition that bedsharing is causally related to SIDS is coherent with theories that respiratory obstruction, re-breathing expired gases, and thermal stress (or overheating), which may also give rise to the release of lethal toxins, are all mechanisms leading to SIDS, in the absence of smoking, alcohol or drugs. Infants placed prone are exposed to similar hazards.

Is the implication in the press release for this article verifiable? Are breastfed, bedsharing babies at *inherent* risk of SIDS events? The answer is equally as simple, but much more informative. No.

Again, factors that put infants' breathing and arousability at risk also increase the risk of SIDS events. The elements of the sleep context that place infants' breathing and arousability at risk are well defined:

✓ Respiratory obstruction (e.g., bedding)

✓ Rebreathing expired gases (i.e., from cover on face)

✓ Thermal stress through overheating (e.g., too many covers)

✓ Physiological vulnerability of arousal (e.g., deep sleep from formula usage)

These authors seem to be arguing that *parenting behavior that can be associated with risk, even if the source of risk is not the behavior, should be stopped* (i.e., bedsharing). This is problematic given that bedsharing is a universal, evolved practice, and is often preferred by parents. In fact, the absence of bedsharing does not eliminate risk of SIDS events.

The diminishing of bedsharing however, is associated with decreases in other behaviors shown to provide protection against SIDS events, such as breastfeeding.

Certainly, without question, a nighttime care context that includes bedsharing and breastfeeding *can include elements that compromise infants' breathing and ability to arouse.* Importantly, we know that breastfeeding not only does not contribute to the risk, but serves to help reduce these risks. See Table 1 whereby bottlefed infants are at a greater risk of a SIDS, regardless of sleep location.

What of Bedsharing?

The authors would have us believe bedsharing *per se* increases the risk of compromising infant breathing and arousability. However, they fail to acknowledge or discuss the fact that there are other factors that influence breathing and arousability, such as bedding, temperature, and premature status (which is correlated with birthweight, but carries with it unique risk factors that must be considered).

Data from Alaska between 1993 and 2004 examined the same question of bedsharing risk, only they also included other known risk factors, such as sleep surface (not just sofa, but the type of bed), and sleeping with a non-caregiver, and compared the data not just to controls (Blabey & Gessner, 2009). Additionally, the comparison group was taken from a state-wide monitoring system that does not focus on answering one day of bedsharing habits, but rather asks parents about usual bedsharing habits.

As such, they most likely had more accurate information on bedsharing than the studies included in the current review. What was found in Alaska? Of the SIDS events that took place while bedsharing, 99% included *at least* one risk factor, and thus the authors conclude that *"infant bedsharing in the absence of other risk factors is not inherently dangerous."*

So, let's stop going around in circles talking about secondary issues and focus on discussion on primary issue: decreasing the risk of SIDS events. If we want to decrease risk of SIDS events, then we must ensure infants are in the best possible situation to support breathing and arousability.

How to do that?

Address Maternal and Infant Health that Reduces Risk

- ✓ Reduce vulnerability by reducing elements that contribute to vulnerability prenatally, i.e., intrauterine exposure to cigarette smoke, premature birth, stressful pregnancy with increased cortisol in blood stream, low birthweight, etc.

- ✓ Reduce vulnerability postnatally by increasing health through breastfeeding, increasing proximity to parent during sleep to protect arousability, increase supportive contexts for new parents to support breastfeeding, infant health, maternal health, etc. This level of support will decrease infant vulnerability, increase infant health, and capacity to arouse.

- ✓ Increase maternal nutrition during pregnancy.

69

Address Nighttime Care Practices to ENSURE Breathing and Arousability

✓ Place infants on back to protect breathing.

✓ Protect infants' breathing and arousal by having infants sleep on firm, flat surface without pillows or toys or blankets.

✓ Protect infants' arousal response by having a cool sleep environment without blankets.

Continue to Monitor Sleep Space

✓ Keep infants in close proximity to parents to assure awareness of compromised breathing or arousal response that may be associated with unobservable variables, such as immature physiological responses.

Despite a long history of efforts to reduce bedsharing, this nighttime-care practice remains to be the preferred practice for many, is increasing in some areas, and provides many protective or health-benefiting outcomes for mothers and infants. Infants' safety at night is compromised when discussions shift from the criteria above to admonitions to sleep separately. A focus on protection, and a discussion of what underlies risk, will be much more successful in reducing risk of SIDS—as well as improving the health context postnatally.

Table 1

Ten Important Risk Factors That Are Not Included in Carpenter et al. (2013)

1	The researchers importantly did not consider whether the bedsharing was planned. Previous research from Venneman (2009) showed **no increased risk in planned bedsharing** (versus unplanned). This is an incredibly important omission.
2	The paper did not consider the effects of the mother smoking during pregnancy, only smoking post birth.
3	Breastfeeding information is too limited to draw conclusions. No difference has been drawn between frequency and percentage of breastfeeds versus formula feeds for those "partially feeding."
4	The paper only considered "illegal drug use." Many postpartum mothers (0-12 weeks after the birth) are prescribed analgesic medication for related birth-induced injuries, including but not limited to Caesarean healing, known to have a sedative effect. This was not considered at all.
5	Prematurity was not considered at all.
6	Parental exhaustion was not considered at all. Some experts suggest this is considered to be less than 4-5 hours of sleep in the past 24-hour period. Other experts advise parents to use their instincts. Parental exhaustion naturally impacts on responsiveness to infant cues.
7	The researchers did not examine the effect of maternal (and paternal) obesity.

8	No differentiation was made between having one or both parents in the bed and importantly the location of the baby. It is advisable that the mother sleeps in between the father and infant. Equally it was not noted if older siblings were also present in the bed.
9	The researchers did not consider fully the impact of alcohol consumption by the father when bed-sharing.
10	No mention was made of whether parents were aware of the risks of bedsharing and how to minimize these before sharing a bed with their infant.

References

Blabey, M.H., & Gessner, B.D. (2009). Infant bed-sharing practices and associated risk factors among births and infant deaths in Alaska. *Public Health Reports, 124,* 527-534.

Carpenter, R., McGarvey, C., Mitchell, E.A., Tappin, D.M., Vennemann, M.M., Smuk, M., & Carpenter, J.R. (2013). Bedsharing when parents do not smoke: Is there a risk of SIDS? An individual level analysis of five major case-control studies. *British Medical Journal Open,* doi:10.1136/bmjopen-2012-002299

Ford, R.P.K., Taylor. B.J., Mitchell, E.A., et al. (1993). Breastfeeding and the risk of sudden infant death syndrome. *International Journal of Epidemiology, 22,* 885-890.

Horne, R.S., Parslow, P.M., Ferens, D., Watts, A.M., & Adamson, T.M. (2004). Comparison of evoked arousability in breast and formula-fed infants. *Archives of Diseases of Childhood, 89*(1), 22-25.

Horta, B.L., Bahl, R., Martinés, J.C., et al. (2007). *Evidence on the long-term effects of breastfeeding: Systematic review and meta-analyses* (pp. 1-57). Geneva: World Health Organization.

Ip, S., Chung, M., Raman, G., Chew, P., Magula, N., DeVine, D., Trikalinos, T, & Lau, J. (2007). Breastfeeding and maternal and infant health outcomes in developed countries. *Evid Rep Technol Assess (FullRep), 153,* 1-186.

Martin, R.M., Gunnell, D., & Smith, G.D. (2005). Breastfeeding in infancy and blood pressure in later life: Systematic review and meta-analysis. *American Journal of Epidemiology, 161,* 15-26.

McVea, K.L., Turner, P.D., & Peppler, D.K. (2000). The role of breastfeeding in sudden infant death syndrome. *Journal of Human Lactation, 16,* 13-20.

Mitchell, E.A., Taylor, B.J., Ford, R.P.K., et al. (1992). Four modifiable and other major risk factors for cot death: The New Zealand study. *Journal of Paediatric of Child Health, 28*(suppl 1), S3-S8.

Mosko, S., Richard, C., & McKenna, J. (1997). Infant arousals during mother-infant bed sharing: implications for infant sleep and sudden infant death syndrome research. *Pediatrics, 100,* 841- 849.

Owen, C.G., Whincup, P.H., Gilg, J.A., et al. (2003). Effect of breast feeding in infancy on blood pressure in later life: Systematic review and meta-analysis. *BMJ, 327,* 1189-1195.

Owen, C.G., Whincup, P.H., Odoki, K., Gilg JA, Cook DG. (2002). Infant feeding and blood cholesterol: a study in adolescents and a systematic review. *Pediatrics, 110,* 597- 608.

Scragg, L.K., Mitchell, E.A., Tonkin, S.L., & Hassall, I.B. (1993). Evaluation of the cot death prevention programme in South Auckland. *New Zealand Medical Journal,* 106, 8-10.

Reprinted from a Praeclarus Press White Paper: *SIDS: Risks and Realities.* A free download is available from Praeclarus Press (www.PraeclarusPress.com). Used with permission.

Chapter 5

The Effect of Feeding Method on Sleep Duration, Maternal Well-Being, and Postpartum Depression

Kathleen Kendall-Tackett
Zhen Cong
Thomas W. Hale

When a breastfeeding mother is depressed—or even at risk for depression—she is often advised to supplement with formula so that she can get more sleep. Results of recent studies suggest, however, that exclusively breastfeeding mothers actually get more sleep than their mixed- or formula-feeding counterparts. The present study examines the relationship between feeding method, maternal well-being, and postpartum depression in a sample of 6,410 mothers of infants 0-12 months of age. Our findings revealed that women who were breastfeeding reported significantly more hours of sleep, better physical health, more energy, and lower rates of depression than mixed- or formula-feeding mothers. Further, there were no significant differences on any measure between mixed- and formula-feeding mothers, suggesting that breastfeeding is a qualitatively different experience than even mixed feeding.

Postpartum depression is a serious health issue that requires an evidence-based response. Unfortunately, mothers sometimes receive advice that is contrary to the available evidence. An example of this is when new mothers are advised to supplement with formula, avoid nighttime feedings, or to wean altogether to lower their risk of depression. One popular book on postpartum depression advises mothers to sleep apart from their infants for 8.4 hours per day, and supplement if necessary to lower their depression risk (Bennett, 2007).

> Sleep in a separate area away from the baby and the adult on duty. Use earplugs and a white noise machine…if necessary. The goal is to make sure that you aren't hearing the baby or other noises so you can achieve uninterrupted sleep (p. 204).

This approach has also been used in a hospital-based program, which allows women at risk for depression to stay in the hospital for up to five days postpartum. In this program, infants room out, breastfeeding women are encouraged to pump and/or use formula for night feedings, and benzodiazepines are used to encourage consistent nighttime sleep onset during the first week (Ross, Murray, & Steiner, 2005).

Unfortunately, people who offer this advice often fail to recognize breastfeeding may be important to the mother, not only as a way to feed her baby—but as a way to help her cope with depression, as this mother describes (Kendall-Tackett, 2010).

> When my first was born, I was completely overwhelmed with the feeling of being her

primary caregiver. I had no family or friends in the area, and my husband had to go back to work when she was 5 or 6 days old. I had panic attacks, and felt like there was no way I was up to being the kind of parent she deserved. Breastfeeding was going well though, and it was often the only thing that I felt like I was doing right...(p. 62).

At first glance, advising mothers to supplement so they can get more rest appears reasonable. But is this approach effective? The evidence, so far, suggests that it is not. In previous studies, it is often the exclusively breastfeeding mothers who get more sleep. For example, a study of 133 new mothers and fathers at three months postpartum found that exclusively breastfeeding mothers slept 40 minutes longer than mixed- or formula-feeding mothers (Doan, Gardiner, Gay, & Lee, 2007).

In another study, "not exclusively breastfeeding" was a risk factor for both sleep problems and postpartum depression in a study of 2,830 women at seven weeks postpartum (Dorheim, Bondevik, Eberhard-Gran, & Bjorvatn, 2009). Consistent with these findings, a recent review of 49 studies found that breastfeeding actually lowers mothers' risk for postpartum depression (Dennis & McQueen, 2009).

Three recent studies found that new mothers' perception of their sleep was a better predictor of fatigue and depression than objective sleep measures. For example, women were significantly more likely to report fatigue if they perceived that their sleep quality was poor and their sleep time was short compared with women who were less fatigued in a sample of 109 postpartum mothers (Rychnovsky & Hunter, 2009).

Another study included 45 new mothers from Melbourne, Australia who were at low risk for postpartum depression (Bei, Milgrom, Ericksen, & Trinder, 2010). The researchers found that perceived sleep quality was more strongly related to postpartum depression than actual sleep time. Similarly, Caldwell and Redeker (2009) found that self-reported sleep accounted for more variance in psychological distress than objective sleep measures in 115 inner-city women from New Haven, Connecticut.

The purpose of the present study is to examine the impact of feeding method on mothers' reported or perceived hours of sleep, maternal fatigue and well-being, and depression in a large sample of mothers in the first postpartum year.

Method

Study Participants

There were 6,410 who participated in the Survey of Mothers' Sleep and Fatigue in 2008-2009, representing 59 countries. (For a full description of the study participants, see Kendall-Tackett, Cong, & Hale, sleep location, this volume).

Sample Recruitment

The sample was recruited via announcements and flyers distributed to WIC Breastfeeding Coordinators, U.S. State Breastfeeding Coalition Coordinators, Lactation Consultants, and La Leche League Leaders. The investigators described the study and asked for assistance in recruiting mothers. Flyers and cards were distributed electronically and via hard copy, with a Web link for the survey. This survey was open to all mothers with babies 0-12 months of age, regardless of feeding method.

Survey Development

The research questions were taken from the 253-item Survey of Mothers' Sleep and Fatigue. The questions were predominately close-ended in format and were developed for this study via open-ended interviews with mothers and feedback from mothers and healthcare professionals.

Survey Questions for Present Analysis

Feeding method was assessed with a series of questions about how and what babies were fed. For the present analysis, an overall summary question was used where mothers selected from one of three options:

Since your baby was born, did you breastfeed, formula feed, or both breast and formula feed?

There were 4,774 mothers who indicated that they were breastfeeding only, 1,125 mothers who were mixed feeding, and 176 mothers who indicated that they were formula feeding.

Mothers were asked to indicate how many hours they slept in an average night. They were also asked to rate their daily energy and overall physical well-being on a five-point Likert scale. Depressed mood, anhedonia and overall depression were assessed via the Patient Health Questionnaire-2, a two-item screening tool for depression (Gjerdingen, Crow, McGovern, Miner, & Center, 2009).

Each symptom (depressed mood and anhedonia) was rated on a scale of 0 to 3. The combined score indicated depression risk, with a higher score indicating greater risk. Means were reported for each of the three feeding groups.

Data Collection

Data were collected via an online survey that was available on the Texas Tech University Department of Pediatrics website. A screening question asked for the baby's age. If the response was 12 months or less, the mother was allowed to continue the survey. The survey and data collection procedure was reviewed and approved by the Texas Tech University School of Medicine Institutional Review Board.

Data Analysis

Data were analyzed using one-way analysis of variance (ANOVA) and X^2 using SPSS version 18.0. Planned contrasts were performed on all ANOVA data comparing breastfeeding mothers to both mixed- and formula-feeding, and comparing mixed- and formula-feeding mothers to each other.

Results & Discussion

Hours of Sleep

Our results indicated that feeding method significantly affected the number of hours mothers reported that they sleep ($F(2)=15.55$, $p<.001$). Planned contrasts revealed that breastfeeding mothers reported significantly more hours of sleep (M=6.61) than either mixed- (M=6.41) or formula-feeding mothers (M=6.3;

p<.001). There was no significant difference between the mixed- and formula-feeding mothers (p>.05).

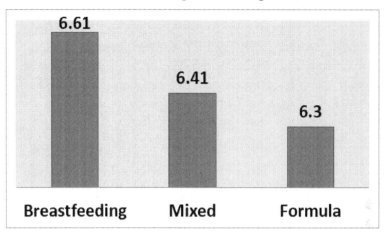

Figure 1: Total number of hours mothers sleep

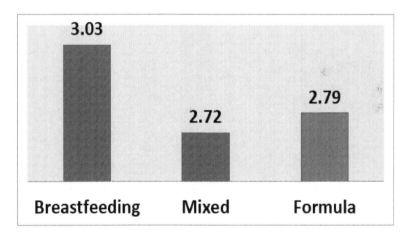

Figure 2: Maternal self-reported energy on most days

Mothers' Physical Well-Being

Consistent with the findings on sleep duration, our results also revealed that feeding method had a significant effect on mothers' reported daily energy

81

(F(2)=46.9, p<.001). Again, planned contrasts revealed that breastfeeding mothers reported significantly more daily energy (M=3.03) than their mixed- (M=2.72) or formula-feeding counterparts (M=2.79; p<.001). There was no significant difference between mixed- and formula-feeding mothers (p>.05). In addition, feeding method influenced mothers' reported overall physical health (F(2)=78.03, p<.001).

Planned contrasts revealed that breastfeeding mothers reported significantly better physical health (M=3.75) than mixed- (M=3.31) or formula-feeding mothers (M=3.44; p<.001). The difference between mixed- and formula-feeding mothers was not significant (p>.05). Finally, a significantly smaller percentage of breastfeeding mothers (37%) reported that the amount of sleep was negatively affecting their health than mixed- (50%) or formula-feeding mothers (49%; $\chi^2(2)=71.79$, p<.001.

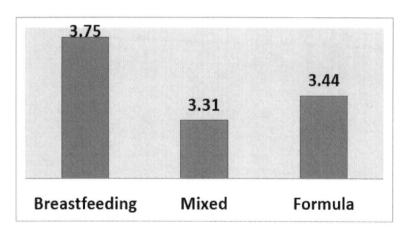

Figure 3: Mothers' overall rating of their physical health

Maternal Depression

Feeding method also influenced mothers' reports of depressed mood, or feeling down, depressed, or hopeless ($F(2)=13.53$, $p<.001$). Planned contrasts revealed that breastfeeding mothers ($M=0.40$) were significantly less likely to report depressed mood than mixed- ($M=0.49$) or formula-feeding mothers ($M=0.59$), and that mixed-feeding mothers were not significantly different than formula-feeding mothers ($p>.05$).

Similarly, feeding method influenced the level of anhedonia ($F(2)=13.27$, $p<.001$), and planned contrasts showed that breastfeeding mothers were significantly less likely to report anhedonia ($M=0.45$) than mixed- ($M=0.55$) or formula-feeding mothers ($M=0.69$, $p<.001$). Mixed-feeding mothers did not show significant difference in anhedonia compared to formula-feeding mothers ($p>.05$).

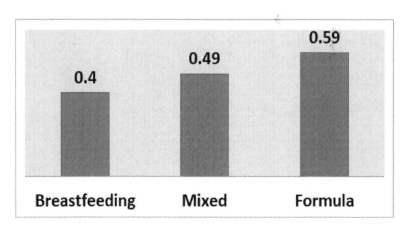

Figure 4: Mothers' reports of feeling down, depressed and hopeless

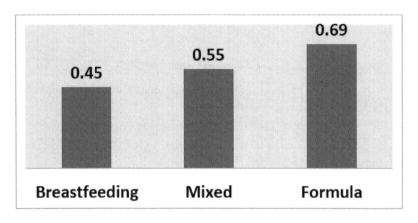

Figure 5: Mothers' reports of anhedonia

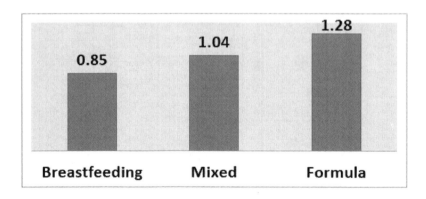

Figure 6: Maternal depression on the PHQ-2

Conclusions

Results in the present study are consistent with findings from previous studies. Breastfeeding mothers reported longer total sleep time, more daily energy, and better physical health than their formula- or mixed-feeding counterparts. They also reported lower rates of depression. Our findings indicate that breastfeeding mothers were qualitatively different than mixed- or formula-feeding mothers on all the variables included in the present study.

Mixed- and formula-feeding mothers did not differ from each other on any of the measures. Exclusive formula feeding—or even supplementing with formula— actually decreased the total number of hours of sleep mothers reported. It also influenced their overall well-being, and increased their risk of depression. Our findings are similar to those of Doan and colleagues (2007), who noted the following.

> Using supplementation as a coping strategy for minimizing sleep loss can actually be detrimental because of its impact on prolactin hormone production and secretion. Maintenance of breastfeeding as well as deep restorative sleep stages may be greatly compromised for new mothers who cope with infant feedings by supplementing in an effort to get more sleep time. (p. 201)

In summary, breastfeeding does not appear to make women more fatigued. On the contrary, the opposite seems to be true. From these data, we concluded that supplementing or weaning actually decreases women's total sleep time, lowers their sense of well-being, and increases their risk of depression.

Given the findings from our study and previous research, we conclude that advising women to supplement, or wean entirely, to lessen their risk of depression is not medically sound. Indeed, if women follow this advice, they may actually increase their risk of both extreme fatigue and depression.

References

Bei, B., Milgrom, J., Ericksen, J., & Trinder, J. (2010). Subjective perception of sleep, but not its objective quality, is associated with immediate postpartum mood disturbances in healthy women. Sleep, 33(4), 531-538.

Bennett, S. (2007). *Postpartum depression for dummies.* Hoboken, NJ: Wiley Publishing.

Caldwell, B. A., & Redeker, N. S. (2009). Sleep patterns and psychological distress in women living in an inner city. *Research in Nursing & Health, 32,* 177-190.

Dennis, C.-L., & McQueen, K. (2009). The relationship between infant-feeding outcomes and postpartum depression: A qualitative systematic review. *Pediatrics, 123,* e736-e751.

Doan, T., Gardiner, A., Gay, C. L., & Lee, K. A. (2007). Breastfeeding increases sleep duration of new parents. *Journal of Perinatal & Neonatal Nursing, 21*(3), 200-206.

Dorheim, S. K., Bondevik, G. T., Eberhard-Gran, M., & Bjorvatn, B. (2009). Sleep and depression in postpartum women: A population-based study. *Sleep, 32*(7), 847-855.

Gjerdingen, D., Crow, S., McGovern, P., Miner, M., & Center, B. (2009). Postpartum depression screening at well-child visits: Validity of a 2-question screen and the PHQ-9. *Annals of Family Medicine, 7*(1), 63-70.

Kendall-Tackett, K. A. (2010). Breastfeeding beats the blues. *Mothering, Sept/Oct*, 60-69.

Kendall-Tackett, K. A., Cong, Z., & Hale, T. W. (2010). Mother-infant sleep locations and nighttime feeding behavior: U.S. data from the Survey of Mothers' Sleep and Fatigue. *Clinical Lactation, 1*(1), 27-30.

Ross, L. E., Murray, B. J., & Steiner, M. (2005). Sleep and perinatal mood disorders: A critical review. *Journal of Psychiatry & Neuroscience, 30*, 247-256.

Rychnovsky, J., & Hunter, L. P. (2009). The relationship between sleep characteristics and fatigue in healthy postpartum women. *Women's Health Issues, 19*, 36-44.

Reprinted from *Clinical Lactation*, 2011, Vol. 2(2), 22-26. Used with permission.

Appendix

Possible Interventions for Very Fatigued New Mothers

Kathleen Kendall-Tackett

Our findings indicate that breastfeeding mothers get more sleep and are less fatigued than mothers who supplement or wean. However, breastfeeding mothers can still be quite fatigued and may need some additional intervention to help prevent or treat depression.

Some Approaches You Might Suggest

Brainstorm with the mother on some strategies to help her cope with fatigue (e.g., encourage her to accept offers of help or access new sources of support).

Treat depression.

Use cognitive-behavioral sleep interventions.

Use sleep medications.

If taking sleep medications, mothers should not bedshare with their infants.

If mother has a trauma history, *The Posttraumatic Insomnia Workbook* will likely be a helpful resource.

Rule Out Physical Conditions

Severe fatigue may also be caused by an underlying physical condition. To rule out physical conditions, the following tests may be helpful.

Blood work to rule out hypothyroidism, anemia, autoimmune disease, low-grade infection, or vitamin D deficiency

TSH, T3, T4, CBC, ESR (Sed rate), vitamin D

Possible sleep study to rule out sleep-breathing and sleep-movement disorders

If limiting feedings does become necessary, a stretch of four to five hours will meet mental health goals, and be less disruptive of breastfeeding.

Section II
The Impact of Sleep-Training and Cry-It-Out Techniques

Chapter 6

Why Cry-It-Out and Sleep-Training Techniques Are Bad for Babes

Kathleen Kendall-Tackett

In 1998, Dr. Dick Krugman, then Editor-in-Chief of the journal *Child Abuse & Neglect*, asked me to write a review of new studies coming out on the neuropsychology of trauma, with a particular focus on the long-term impact of childhood abuse. I was happy to do it. It was an exciting time in the child maltreatment/trauma field.

With new technology, researchers could finally study living human brains. This technology opened up whole new worlds, and I had a chance to summarize these findings for the major journal in my field (Kendall-Tackett, 2000).

The article took months to write. Since research in this field was so new, many of the findings were contradictory. For example, the physiological footprint of major depression was the exact opposite of the footprint

93

for posttraumatic stress disorder (PTSD). How could that be? It was common for one person to have both.

Researchers eventually developed better models that helped us understand these apparently contradictory findings. But in those first few years, they were hard to understand. One finding, however, was remarkably consistent across studies: chronic stress was bad for the brain.

This was true for adults. And it was especially true for children under the age of five, whose brains are malleable, and therefore highly vulnerable to stress. As Bruce Perry found, ongoing childhood stress could permanently alter the way children's brains worked.

Robert Sapolsky (1996) authored one of the classic articles on the effects of stress in the journal *Science*: Why stress is bad for the brain. In this article, he described the impact of the stress hormone cortisol on the hippocampus, the section of the brain involved in learning and memory. In *in vitro* studies, dripping cortisol on hippocampal cells made them shrink. In living human beings, those who experienced ongoing chronic stress or depression (which elevated cortisol levels), had smaller hippocampi than those without stress or depression. Doug Bremner and others have found a similar pattern with combat vets and sexual abuse survivors with PTSD (Bremner, 2006). There were many other studies with similar findings. But the bottom line is this: chronically elevated cortisol levels harm brain cells.

So imagine my shock when I first learned that generally well-meaning parents were deliberately subjecting their babies to routines that chronically elevated their cortisol levels. The parents wanted to train their babies to sleep, or to be independent.

94

Some of these approaches are worse than others, and the milder forms will probably not cause long-term harm if they occur in the context of overall responsive parenting. I'm sure that parents who tried these approaches thought they were doing the right thing. However, if you understand the physiology, how could chronically raising babies' cortisol levels by not responding to them possibly be the right thing? (See Narvaez, Dangers of Crying It Out, this volume.)

Although it has not been specifically studied, it is plausible that sleep training and cry-it-out techniques could also harm breastfeeding. Breastfeeding depends on mothers responding to their babies' cues. Historically, we have seen the disasterous effects of scheduled feeding on breastfeeding. Sleep training, especially when it involves ignoring infants' cries, could have the same effect. Mothers who are told to ignore their babies' cries in some instances will find it more difficult to be responsive to their infants in other instances. This is a case of culture overriding a mother's hard-wired response to her baby.

Spacing out feedings, or stopping night feedings at some arbitrary age, will have a direct impact on a mother's milk production, possibly opening the door to low milk-supply, decreased weight gain, increased supplementation, and even failure to thrive.

In 2013, there were two widely publicized studies, with wide news coverage, that advocated sleep training and "cry it out" techniques. These approaches are vestiges from Behaviorism, a school of thought that dominated American Psychology from the 1920s to the early 1960s. The idea behind sleep training, etc., is that if you respond to crying you are just "reinforcing" it— meaning that you are increasing the likelihood that it will happen again. As the chapters in Section II describe, subsequent anthropological and psychological research has demonstrated the opposite to be true. Babies whose cries are answered in infancy tend to cry less in later infancy and beyond.

In addition, chronic stress in infancy and early childhood has been identified as a major contributor to adult health problems. In 2009, Jack Shonkoff and colleagues published a major review in the *Journal of the American Medical Association* that stated that "adult disease prevention begins with reducing early toxic stress." Considering the state of Americans' health, this is something we should take quite seriously. A recent report from the Institute of Medicine (2013) noted the following:

> For many years, Americans have been dying at younger ages than people in almost all other high-income countries. This disadvantage has been getting worse for three decades, especially among women. Not only are their lives shorter, but Americans also have a longstanding pattern of poorer health that is strikingly consistent and pervasive over the life course.

One way we can improve the health of the next generation is to challenge the hegemony of the cry-it-out advocates. We need to stand by the mothers we serve as they make the decision to defy cultural norms and respond to their babies. The health of the next generation depends on it.

References

Bremner, J.D. (2006). Stress and brain atrophy. *CNS and Neurological Disorders Drug Targets, 5*(5), 503-512.

Institute of Medicine. (2013). *U.S. health in international perspective: Shorter lives, poorer health.* Retrieved from: http://www.iom.edu/~/media/Files/ Report%20Files/2013/US-HealthInternational- Perspective/USHealth_Intl_PerspectiveRB.pdf

Kendall-Tackett, K. A. (2000). Physiological correlates of childhood abuse: Chronic hyperarousal in PTSD, depression, and irritable bowel syndrome. *Child Abuse & Neglect, 24,* 799-810.

Sapolsky, R.M. (1996). Why stress is bad for your brain. *Science, 273,* 749-750.

Shonkoff, J. P., Boyce, W. T., & McEwen, B. S. (2009). Neuroscience, molecular biology, and the childhood roots of health disparities: Building a new framework for health promotion and disease prevention. *JAMA, 301*(21), 2252-2259.

Reprinted from *Clinical Lactation,* 2013, Vol. 4(2), 53-54. Used with permission.

Chapter 7

Dangers of "Crying It Out"
Damaging Children and Their Relationships for the Long-term
Darcia Narvaez

Letting babies "cry it out" is an idea that has been around since at least the 1880s, when the field of medicine was in a hullaballoo about germs and transmitting infection, and so took to the notion that babies should rarely be touched (see Blum, 2002, for a great review of this time period and attitudes towards childrearing).

In the 20th century, behaviorist John Watson (1928), interested in making psychology a hard science, took up the crusade against affection as president of the American Psychological Association. He applied the mechanistic paradigm of Behaviorism to childrearing, warning about the dangers of too much mother love.

The 20th century was the time when "men of science" were assumed to know better than mothers, grandmothers, and families about how to raise a child.

99

Too much kindness to a baby would result in a whiney, dependent, failed human being. Funny how "the experts" got away with this with no evidence to back it up! Instead there is evidence all around (then and now) showing the opposite to be true.

A government pamphlet from the time recommended that "mothering meant holding the baby quietly, in tranquility-inducing positions," and that "the mother should stop immediately if her arms feel tired" because "the baby is never to inconvenience the adult." Babies older than six months "should be taught to sit silently in the crib; otherwise, he might need to be constantly watched and entertained by the mother, a serious waste of time." (See Blum, 2002.)

Don't these attitudes sound familiar? A parent reported to me recently that he was encouraged to let his baby cry herself to sleep so he "could get his life back."

With neuroscience, we can confirm what our ancestors took for granted: that letting babies get distressed is a practice that can damage children and their relational capacities in many ways for the long term. We know now that leaving babies to cry is a good way to make a less intelligent and healthy, but more anxious, uncooperative and alienated person, who can pass the same—or worse—traits on to the next generation.

The discredited view sees the baby as an interloper into the life of the parents, an intrusion who must be controlled by various means so the adults can live their lives without too much bother. Perhaps we can excuse this attitude and ignorance because at the time extended families were being broken up, and new parents had to figure out how to deal with babies on their own: an unnatural condition for humanity. We have heretofore raised children in extended families. The parents always shared care with multiple adult relatives.

According to this discredited view, completely ignorant of human development, the child "has to be taught to be independent." We can confirm now that forcing "independence" on a baby leads to greater dependence. Instead, giving babies what they need leads to greater independence later.

In anthropological reports of small-band hunter-gatherers, parents took care of every need of babies and young children. Toddlers felt confident enough (and so did their parents) to walk into the bush on their own (see *Hunter-Gatherer Childhoods*, edited by Hewlett & Lamb, 2005).

Ignorant advisors then—and now—encourage parents to condition the baby to expect needs NOT to be met on demand, whether feeding or comforting. It's assumed that the adults should "be in charge" of the relationship. Certainly this might foster a child that doesn't ask for as much help and attention (withdrawing into depression and going into stasis—or even wasting away), but it is more likely to foster a whiny, unhappy, aggressive, and/or demanding child: one who has learned that one must scream to get needs met. A deep sense of insecurity is likely to stay with them for the rest of their lives.

The fact is that caregivers who habitually respond to the needs of the baby before the baby gets distressed, preventing crying, are more likely to have children who are independent than the opposite (e.g., Stein & Newcomb, 1994). Soothing care is best from the outset. Once patterns get established, it's much harder to change them.

101

We should understand the mother and child as a mutually responsive dyad. They are a symbiotic unit that make each other healthier and happier in mutual responsiveness. This expands to other caregivers too.

One strangely popular notion still around today is to let babies "cry it out" when they are left alone, isolated in cribs or other devices. This comes from a misunderstanding of child and brain development.

1. Babies grow from being held. Their bodies get dysregulated when they are physically separated from caregivers.

2. Babies indicate a need through gesture and eventually, if necessary, through crying. Just as adults reach for liquid when thirsty, children search for what they need in the moment. Just as adults become calm once the need is met, so do babies.

3. There are many long-term effects of under care, or need-neglect, in babies (e.g., Dawson et al., 2000).

What does "crying it out" actually do to the baby and to the dyad?

Neurons die. When the baby is stressed, the toxic hormone cortisol is released. It's a neuron killer. A full-term baby (40 to 42 weeks), with only 25% of its brain developed, is undergoing rapid brain growth. The brain grows, on average, three times as large by the end of the first year (and head size growth in the first year is a sign of intelligence, e.g., Gale et al., 2006).

Who knows what neurons are not being connected, or being wiped out during times of extreme stress? What deficits might show up years later from such regular distressful experience?

Disordered stress reactivity can be established as a pattern for life not only in the brain with the stress-response system, but also in the body through the vagus nerve, a nerve that affects functioning in multiple systems (e.g., digestion). For example, prolonged distress in early life, resulting in a poorly functioning vagus nerve, is related to disorders, such as irritable bowel syndrome (Stam et al., 1997). (See more about how early stress is toxic for lifelong health from the recent Harvard report, *The Foundations of Lifelong Health are Built in Early Childhood*).

Self-regulation is undermined. The baby is absolutely dependent on caregivers for learning how to self-regulate. Responsive care—meeting the baby's needs before he gets distressed—tunes the body and brain up for calmness. When a baby gets scared, and a parent holds and comforts him, the baby builds expectations for soothing, which get integrated into the ability to self-comfort.

Babies don't self-comfort in isolation. If they are left to cry alone, they learn to shut down in face of extensive distress—stop growing, stop feeling, stop trusting (Henry & Wang, 1998).

Trust is undermined. As Erik Erikson pointed out, the first year of life is a sensitive period for establishing a sense of trust in the world, the world of caregiver, and the world of self. When a baby's needs are met without distress, the child learns that the world is a trustworthy place, that relationships are supportive, and

103

that the self is a positive entity that can get its needs met.

When a baby's needs are dismissed or ignored, the child develops a sense of mistrust of relationships and the world. And self-confidence is undermined. The child may spend a lifetime trying to fill the inner emptiness.

Caregiver responsiveness to the needs of the baby is related to most—if not all—positive child outcomes. In our work, caregiver responsiveness is related to intelligence, empathy, lack of aggression or depression, self-regulation, and social competence. Because responsiveness is so powerful, we have to control for it in our studies of other parenting practices and child outcomes.

The importance of caregiver responsiveness is common knowledge in developmental psychology. Lack of responsiveness, which "crying it out" represents, can result in the opposite of the aforementioned positive outcomes.

The "cry it out" approach seems to have arisen as a solution to the dissolution of extended family life in the 20th century. The vast wisdom of grandmothers was lost in the distance between households with children, and those with the experience and expertise about how to raise them well. The wisdom of keeping babies happy was lost between generations.

But isn't it normal for babies to cry?

No. A crying baby in our ancestral environment would have signaled predators to tasty morsels. So our evolved parenting practices alleviated baby distress and precluded crying except in emergencies. Babies are built to expect the equivalent of an "external womb" after birth (see Allan Schore, specific references below). What is the external womb? — being held constantly, breastfed on demand, and needs met quickly.

These practices are known to facilitate good brain and body development. When babies display discomfort, it signals that a need is not getting met, a need of their rapidly growing systems.

What does extensive baby crying signal?

It shows the lack of experience, knowledge, and/ or support of the baby's caregivers. To remedy a lack of information in us all, I listed a good set of articles about all the things that a baby's cry can signal. We can all educate ourselves about what babies need and the practices that alleviate baby crying. We can help one another to keep it from happening as much as possible.

For Further Reading

Blum, D. (2002). *Love at Goon Park: Harry Harlow and the science of affection.* New York: Berkeley Publishing (Penguin).

Dawson, G., et al. (2000). The role of early experience in shaping behavioral and brain development and its implications for social policy. *Development and Psychopathology, 12*(4), 695-712.

Gale, C.R., O'Callaghan, F.J., Bredow, M., Martyn, C.N., and the Avon Longitudinal Study of Parents and Children Study Team. (2006). The influence of head growth in fetal life, infancy, and childhood on intelligence at the ages of 4 and 8 years. *Pediatrics, 118*(4), 1486-1492.

Henry, J.P., & Wang, S. (1998). Effects of early stress on adult affili¬ative behavior. *Psychoneuroendocrinology, 23*(8), 863-875.

Hewlett, B., & Lamb, M. (2005). *Hunter-gatherer childhoods.* New York: Aldine.

Meaney, M.J. (2001). Maternal care, gene expression, and the transmission of individual differences in stress reactivity across generations. *Annual Review of Neuroscience, 24,* 1161-1192.

Narvaez, D., Panksepp, J., Schore, A., & Gleason, T. (Eds.) (2013). *Evolution, early experience and human development: From research to practice and policy.* New York: Oxford University Press.

Schore, A.N. (1997). Early organization of the nonlinear right brain and development of a predisposition to psychiatric disorders. *Development and Psychopathology, 9,* 595-631.

Schore, A.N. (2000). Attachment and the regulation of the right brain. *Attachment & Human Development, 2,* 23-47.

Schore, A.N. (2001). The effects of early relational trauma on right brain development, affect regulation, and infant mental health. *Infant Mental Health Journal, 22,* 201-269.

Stein, J. A., & Newcomb, M. D. (1994). Children's internalizing and externalizing behaviors and maternal health problems. *Journal of Pediatric Psychology, 19*(5), 571-593.

UNICEF (2007). *Child poverty in perspective: An overview of child well-being in rich countries, a comprehensive assessment of the lives and well-being of children and adolescents in the economically advanced nations,* Report Card 7. Florence, Italy: United Nations

Children's Fund Innocenti Research Centre.

U.S. Department of Health and Human Services, Substance Abuse and Mental Health Services Administration. (1999). *Mental health: A report of the Surgeon General.* Rockville, MD: Center for Mental Health Services, National Institutes of Health, National Institute of Mental Health.

Watson, J. B. (1928). *Psychological care of infant and child.* New York: W. W. Norton Company.

WHO/WONCA (2008). *Integrating mental health into primary care: A global perspective.* Geneva and London: World Health Organiza¬tion and World Organization of Family Doctors.

Reprinted from *Clinical Lactation*, 2012, Vol. 3(1), 32-35. Used with permission.

Chapter 8

Why Not "Crying It Out"
Part 1
The Science that Tells Us that Responsiveness Is Key

Patrice Marie Miller
Michael Lamport Commons

Considerable research, both experimental research with animals and research with humans, now documents the detrimental effects of early stress on brain development. These effects can occur not just in response to intense and repetitive stressful situations, but with some probability may also occur in situations of parenting that is not responsive. In this context, this chapter addresses the biologically and ethologically based reasons that crying is detrimental to infants' development—negatively impacting neurological structures, stress responses, physical health, and socioemotional well-being.

From birth, human infants have a limited ability to control their environment. If distressed, they will usually cry, but it is not up to them what happens in response to that cry. Infants have limited self-soothing abilities (Emde, 1998), and are reliant upon an appropriate response from caregivers. Of course, as they develop, their response repertoires increase so that they may be responded to more effectively, and their own coping and self-soothing behaviors also develop.

It remains true, however, that the successful development of an infant, and even a young child, is due to an intricate, interactive process between that child and its caregivers. In that context, the number and kinds of stressful events (or "stressors") that an infant encounters in the course of a day is a factor that may have a major effect on their development.

While caregivers cannot totally eliminate stressors, they can have major control over the number and kinds of stressful events. Caregivers can impact infants' experiences of stressors as well by being present, holding, and/or otherwise consoling an infant during a stressful event.

The purpose of this chapter is to examine a large body of evidence on the effect of early stressors on development. In "Why Not 'Crying It Out,' Part 2," we examine common care practices in some cultures, such as northern Euro-American cultures, that can produce excessive stress for some infants and young children. What mitigates against these stressors is re-adopting practices familiar to professionals and protective of infants' development.

These practices can include co-sleeping or parent-settling sleep, increasing the rate of bodily contact and holding, and other responsive care behaviors. The argument for these mitigating practices will be presented based on this evidence.

Evidence for the Negative Effects of Stress on Development

The literature on the effects of early stressful events on development has been growing by leaps and bounds for roughly the last 15 years. The evidence for these effects comes from two sources: (a) experimental research on animals, such as rats or monkeys, which combines controlled exposure to stressful events with examination of brain changes and behavior, and (b) research involving human children and adults that relates different kinds of early experiences to brain changes and/or to behavior in a correlational fashion. Each will be briefly reviewed in turn.

Effects of Stressful Events on Brain Development in Non-Human Animals

Recognizing that we are mammals is an important step in helping to understand the importance of early care. Because of the nature of development, researchers and scientists are able to explore the connection between care and brain development—particularly with regard to early care and the impact on later behavior—more readily than they might if working with new parents and infants.

The information gathered has provided substantial support that solidifies the importance of early care. The strength of this support is presented here as a means of assuring professionals of the value and importance of the sleep and care routines often recommended.

Biological Importance of Maternal Care

A number of investigators have studied the long-term effects of stressful early rearing conditions in nonhuman animals. Some of the early research in this area provides a clear look into the importance of care in shaping later behavior. In their research using rhesus monkeys, Suomi and colleagues (1987; 1991) have investigated the differential effects of being reared by their mother in the traditional way, or by being separated from the mother and being reared by peers.

Peer-reared monkeys seemed to develop relatively normal social behavior as long as they were in familiar settings. When exposed to stressors, such as separations from other monkeys, however, they exhibited much more behavioral disruption, and a greater activation of the hypothalamic-pituitary-adrenal axis and other systems involved in dealing with stress.

Suomi (1987) also reported that there were important individual differences in the reactivity of different individual monkeys, with roughly 20% of them being highly reactive to stress. Even when mother-reared, these monkeys showed much more extreme behavioral and physiological reactions to stressful situations. They might, for example, appear fearful in novel situations and have heightened levels of cortisol and ACTH (adrenocorticotropic hormone).

These patterns of behavior, both from monkeys who were reared by peers, and in the highly reactive monkeys, have been found to persist into later development.

Stressful Environments and Caregiving

Research continues to support these earlier findings. In an extensive review of studies with rodents and also non-human primates, Sánchez, Ladd, and Plotsky (2001) summarized a great deal of evidence showing the role of stress in early rearing for both rodents and primates. What was evident through the review was that early adverse experiences, including prenatal stress or illness in the mother and separations from the mother, for either brief or extended periods of time, changes the way that the limbic-hypothalamic-pituitary-adrenal (LHPA) axis is regulated.

While the negative effects on this stress-regulation system have been shown to vary somewhat in different individuals and during different periods of development, across all the species studied, a number of similar effects were seen. These included: "increase in fearfulness and anxiety-like behavior, and...deficits in social behavior, sexual behavior, and cognitive performance" (p. 440, Sánchez et al.).

One interesting finding that is also part of this literature is that for rodents, certain caregiving behaviors from the mother, specifically licking and grooming of the pups during the first 10 days, led to reduced levels of plasma adrenocorticotropic hormone, as well as other responses to stress (Liu et al., 1997). According to the authors, an important function of maternal behavior is to "program" the regulation of the LHPA axis. We will argue (below) that the same is true in humans.

Research on Effects of Stressful Events on Human Behavior and Brain Development

The long-term effects of early stress experiences have been found to be much the same in humans. Sources of stress examined in regard to infants' well-being have included studies regarding trauma or abuse in infancy (e.g., Essex, Klein, Cho & Kalin, 2002; Ito, Teicher, Glod, & Ackerman, 1998; Perry, 1997).

Other literature discusses stressors that a significant number of children are exposed to, including low socioeconomic status (Lupien et al., 2000), stress due to maternal depression (e.g., Ashman et al., 2002; Essex et al., 2002), and simply "low-quality maternal behavior" (Hane & Fox, 2006). This body of research has been summarized both by the National Scientific Council on the Development of the Child (2005), and Shonkoff and colleagues (2012).

These latter reports, in particular, include evidence showing that there are short- and long-term effects on both mental and physical health when children grow up in stressful environments. Exposure to chronic stress seems to be associated with physical disorders (for example, cardiovascular disease, cancer), and also psychological disorders, such as depression and anxiety (see McEwen & Seeman, 1999).

In some studies, exposure to high amounts of cortisol that is released in response to stressors has been shown to result in damage to the hippocampus (involved in learning and memory; e.g., Lupien et al., 1998), and the amygdala (involved in the processing of emotions; e.g., Wolterink et al., 2001).

Why This Is Important

During the first years of life, a child's experiences of stress will begin to shape the functioning of their stress-response systems. When infancy is marked by acute or chronic stress experiences, the impact on this system can be irreversible, leading to the development of an overactive, intense response system to stress, or a dampening of response (Gunnar, 1998).

Infants' first experiences are crucial for the developing hypothalamic-pituitary-adrenocortical (HPA) axis because this system is very responsive to stimulation. This can be seen by parents and care providers in infants' experiences of everyday events, even minor events such as being undressed. In her work, Gunnar has found that infants can experience elevations in cortisol during these caretaking activities (Gunnar, 1992). Some infants may be more sensitive to these events based on being temperamentally more reactive. The findings of this kind of research are very much echoed in the findings from the research reported by Sánchez, Ladd, and Plotsky (2001), among many others.

The sum of this research, conducted across different populations and using many different methodologies, suggests that exposure to stressors early in life can rearrange certain systems in the brain, particularly the limbic-hypothalamic-pituitary-adrenal (LHPA) axis, which responds to stress.

Dysregulation of the LHPA axis is related to both physiological changes that are related to physical illnesses, and to psychopathology (see Caldji, et al., 2001; DeBellis, et al., 1994; Heims, Owens, Plotsky, & Nemeroff, 1997; Young, Abelson, Curtis & Nesse, 1997). Most importantly, these effects appear to be present along a continuum of stressor severity, from severe stressors such as separations from the mother, to those that are less severe.

What Kind of Model Should We Use When Thinking about the Effects of Stress?

In thinking about the possible effects of stressful events, it is important for parents, and those working directly with parents, to have an explanatory model that fits the results that are described. With such a model, it would be possible to address some of the typical early care questions parents may raise.

Questions might include whether an equally severe form of stress could be expected to have the same kinds of effects on all individuals? Are these characteristics of individuals, or are there other events that might mitigate these possible effects?

A Model Helpful for Working with Families

Currently, one can best describe the explanatory models of the field as consisting of multilevel-dynamic systems accounts, in which characteristics of individuals, as well as contexts, are both important in understanding outcomes of development.

According to Sameroff (2010), the self consists of interacting psychological and biological processes, resulting in a biopsychological self-system. In this system, psychological processes include social behaviors, cognitive and emotional intelligence, and mental health, while the biological processes include the nervous system and neuroendocrine systems among other processes.

The system then interacts within the settings of family, school, etc. This transactional model of development suggests a system of back and forth influences between the biology of the individual, and the characteristics of the various environments that the individual interacts within. That is, a biological change may affect an individual's behavior, which might then elicit changes in the environment. That changed environment can then impinge on the biological systems that started the cycle in the first place.

These transactions have to be considered over time, and in the context of how the individual is changing. In general, in examining the influence of negative events, such as stress, research has relied on what is called the diathesis-stress model (e.g., see paper by Caspi and co-authors, 2002), in which a biological vulnerability of some kind is shown to worsen the effects of stress.

Model Application

This model helps to explain what professionals know from working with families. However, in this application, the professional now has the tools and explanations to help mothers understand the importance of seeing their infants as individuals, and their relationship with the infants as impacting their system of interaction.

A second new development in the field helps to make even more clear the importance of the interaction between mothers and infants—a relationship that the professional has the capacity to discuss with mothers. This development is the recognition of a more general "differential susceptibility" to experiences (Belsky, 1997). For example, in studies of the effects of children's early experiences in child care, few overall negative effects of child care were found.

When researchers focused only on children with negative temperaments, however, they found that these children were both more negatively affected by low-quality care environments, and more positively affected by high-quality care environments (Pluess & Belsky, 2009).

Keeping these models in mind will be useful when considering whether some infant care practices, that are used by many parents in this and other cultures, could cause significant enough stress to change an infant's developmental course to one that is less than optimal.

References

Ashman, S. B. Dawson, G., Panagiotides, H., Yamada, E. & Wilkinson, C. W. (2002). *Development and Psychopathology, 14*(2), 333-349.

Belsky, J. (1997). Variation in susceptibility to rearing influences: An evolutionary argument. *Psychological Inquiry*, 8, 182–186.

Caldji, C., Liu, D., Sharma, S., Diorio, J., Francis, D., Meaney, M., & Plotsky, P. M. (2001). Development of individual differences in behavioral and endocrine responses to stress: Role of the postnatal environment. In B. S. Ewen (Ed.), *Handbook of physiology: Coping with the environment* (pp. 271-292). New York: Oxford University Press.

DeBellis, M. D., Chrousos, G. P., Dom, L. D., Burke, L., Helmers, K., Kling, M.A., Trickett, P.K., & Putnam, F. W. (1994). Hypothalamic pituitary adrenal dysregulation in sexually abused girls. *Journal of Clinical Endocrinology and Metabolism, 78,* 249-255.

Emde, R. N. (1998). Early emotional development: New modes of thinking for research and intervention. In J. G. Warhol & S. P. Shelov (Eds.), *New perspectives in early emotional development.* Johnson & Johnson Pediatric Institute, Ltd.

Essex, M. J., Klein, M. H., Cho, E., & Kalin, N. H. (2002). Maternal stress beginning in infancy may sensitize children to later stress exposure: Effects on cortisol and behavior. *Biological Psychiatry, 52,* 776-784.

Gunnar, M. R. (1992). Reactivity of the hypothalamic-pituitary-adrenocortical system to stressors in normal infants and children. *Pediatrics (Suppl), 90*(3), 491-497.

Gunnar, M. R. (1998). Quality of early care and buffering of neuroendocrine stress reactions: Potential effects on the developing human brain. *Preventive Medicine, 27,* 208-211.

Hane, A. A., & Fox, N. A. (2006). Ordinary variations in maternal caregiving influence human infants' stress reactivity. *Psychological Science, 17*(6), 550-556.

Heim, C., Owens, M. J., Plotsky, P. M., & Nemeroff, C. B. (1997). The role of early adverse life events in the etiology of depression and posttraumatic stress disorder: Focus on corticotropin-releasing factor. *Annals of the New York Academy of Sciences USA, 821,* 194-207.

Ito, Y., Teicher, M. H., Glod, C. A., & Ackerman, E. (1998). Preliminary evidence for aberrant cortical development in abused children: A quantitative EEG study. *Journal of Neuropsychiatry and Clinical Neurosciences, 10,* 298-307.

Liu, D., Diorio, J., Tannenbaum, B., Caldji, C., Francis, D., Freedman, A., Sharma, S., Pearson, D., Plotsky, P. M., & Meaney, M. J. (1997). Maternal care, hippocampal glucocorticoid receptors, and hypothalamic-pituitary-adrenal responses to stress. *Science, 277* (Issue 5332), 1659-1663.

Luecken, L. J. (1998). Childhood attachment and low experiences affect adult cardiovascular and cortisol function. *Psychosomatic Medicine, 60,* 765-772.

Lupien, S. J., King, S., Meaney, M. J., & McEwen, B. S. (2001). Can poverty get under your skin? Basal cortisol levels and cognitive function in children from low and high socioeconomic status. *Developmental Psychopathology, 13,* 653–676.

McEwen, B. S., & Seeman, T. (1999). Protective and damaging effects of mediators of stress: Elaborating and testing the concepts of allostatis and allostatic load. In N. E. Adler, M. Marmot, B. S. McEwen, & J. Steward (Eds.), Socioeconomic status and health in industrial nations: Social, psychological and biological pathways. *Annals of the New York Academy of Sciences, 896,* 30-47.

National Council on the Developing Child (2005). *Excessive stress disrupts the architecture of the developing brain.* Working paper No. 3. Retrieved from: http://www.developingchild.net/reports.shtml.

Perry, B. D. (1997). Incubated in terror: Neurodevelopmental factors in the "Cycle of Violence." In J. Osofsky (Ed.), *Children, youth and violence: The search for solutions* (pp. 124-148). New York: Guilford.

Pluess, M., & Belsky, J. (2009). Differential susceptibility to rearing experience: The case of childcare. *Journal of Child Psychology and Psychiatry and Allied Disciplines, 50*(4), 396–404.

Rosenblum, L. A., Coplan, J. D., Friedman, S., Bassoff, T., Gorman, J. M., & Andrews, M. W. (1994). Adverse early experiences affect noradrenergic and serotonergic functioning in adult primates. *Biological Psychiatry, 35,* 221-227.

Sameroff, A. (2010). A unified theory of development: A dialectic integration of nature and nurture. *Child Development, 81,* 6-22.

Sánchez, M. M., Ladd, C. O., & Plotsky, P.M. (2001). Early adverse experience as a developmental risk factor for later psychopathology: Evidence from rodent and primate models. *Development and Psychopathology, 13,* 419-449.

Shonkoff, J. P., & Garner, A.S., The Committee on Psychosocial Aspects of Child and Family Health, Committee on Early Childhood, Adoption and Dependent Care, and Section on Developmental and Behavioral Pediatrics, Siegel, B. S., Dobbins, M. I, Earls, M. F., McGuinn, L., Pascoe, J., & Wood, D. L. (2012). The lifelong effects of early childhood adversity and toxic stress. *Pediatrics, 129*(1), 232-246.

Suomi, S. J. (1987). Genetic and environmental contributions to individual differences in rhesus monkey biobehavioral development. In N. Krasnegor, E. Blass, M. Hofer, and W. Smotherman (Eds.), *Perinatal development: A psychobiological perspective* (pp. 397-420). New York: Academic Press.

Suomi, A. J. (1991). Early stress and adult emotional reactivity in rhesus monkeys. In G. R. Bock & J. Whelan (Eds.), *Ciba Foundation Symposium: Childhood environment and adult disease.* New York: Wiley.

Wolterink, G., Lisette, E. W., Daenen, P. M., Dubbeldam, S., Mirgam, A. F., Gerrits, M., van Rijn, R., Cruse, C. G., Van Der Haijden, J. A. M., & Van Ree, J. M. (2001). Early amygdala damage in the rat as a model for neurodevelopmental psychopathological disorders. *European Neuropsychopharamacology, 11*(1), 51-59.

Young, E. A., Abelson, J. L., Curtis, C. G., & Nesse, R. M. (1997). Childhood adversity and vulnerability to mood and anxiety disorders. *Depression Anxiety, 5,* 66-72.

Reprinted from *Clinical Lactation,* 2013, Vol. 4(2), 57-61. Used with permission.

Chapter 9

Why Not "Crying It Out" Part 2

Can Certain Infant Care Practices Cause Excessive Stress?

Patrice Marie Miller
Michael Lamport Commons

Understanding the importance of responsiveness is an essential foundation for communicating with parents about early care. Helping parents create healthy, responsive environments may benefit from looking at some common parenting practices and how they may impact infants' development. The role of stress experiences is an essential consideration when choosing care. What practices may be more risky for infants and which may be more protective is the focus of Part 2.

In Part 1 of "Why Not 'Crying It Out'," we reviewed the science forming the foundation for the importance of communicating to mothers about how they provide early care. This science helps to show

how early care will impact infants' developing brains and stress responses, how this aspect of neurological development will impact later behavior.

The next important question to be answered for professionals, and then shared with parents, is whether there are some relatively routine practices used by parents in the United States (and some other countries) that may be stressful enough to affect infants' development. Based on the science then—the question is whether these practices could produce changes in infants' brains and behaviors in the ways indicated by the research on stress and its effects.

Explored here are practices often associated with crying it out—practices such as putting infants to bed by themselves, and allowing them to cry instead of picking them up when they do not fall asleep; or allowing infants to cry and not picking them up when they wake up at night.

Other similar practices marked by parents' non-response would include showing a relative lack of response to crying during the day time (so as not to "spoil" the baby), not holding or touching the baby very much, and so on. We will explore these practices from the framework of parent- and child-centered practices (Miller & Commons, 2010), tying these different practices back to the research reviewed above, and examining the impact of these practices on children's development.

Parent-Centered Versus Child-Centered Parenting with Infants

Child-Centered Practices and Infant Sleep

Child-centered parenting involves learning to read the cues of the infant, and responding appropriately to those cues. Thus, child-centered parenting practices can encompass a variety of parenting strategies, such as feeding in a manner that is responsive to infant cues, and being highly responsive to crying, or pre-crying, as well as to other cues, co-sleeping or responding to infants during nighttime care, and emphasizing bodily contact more than physical separation. A main result of such practices is a reduction in stressful situations for the infant.

In regard to sleeping patterns, practices in which parents attend to infant signaling can provide a child-centered focus. Additionally, co-sleeping can be viewed as child-centered as this nighttime care practice allows for much faster responsiveness to infant cues. With this practice, infants who co-sleep will not be exposed to the extended crying that can occur when they are left alone to fall asleep on their own, or when their parents do not retrieve them from their crib at night.

Having infants co-sleep or sleep in close proximity to parents, rather than in a physically separate crib or a crib in a separate room, can greatly mitigate or completely eliminate problems that a parent may have in getting their infant to sleep, and in dealing with night wakefulness (Miller & Commons, 2010). In addition, mother-infant sleep positions can lead to safer sleep (McKenna & McDade, 2005), as well as enhance the quality of sleep (Teti, Kim, Mayer, & Countermine, 2010),

125

and offer a greater probability of continued breastfeeding (McKenna & McDade, 2005).

Child-Centered Practices and Infants' Crying

One important area of behavior to examine is how quickly and how often mothers and other caregivers respond to infant crying. Infants who are less often responded to, or who are not responded to very quickly, are likely to experience more stress.

This topic overlaps somewhat with the topic of infant holding, since picking up and holding would be a frequent response to crying, along with other behaviors. The distinction is that here, what is being looked at is the presence of a contingent response. The research on responsiveness to crying has not looked at the specific nature of responses to crying, only at how often parents (usually mothers) respond.

This topic was discussed in some detail in Miller and Commons (2010), so here we will present just a summary. Two opposing points of view have been put forward. One, more on the child-centered side, has suggested that responding to infant crying in a timely and contingent fashion reduces the rate of such crying (Bell & Ainsworth, 1972).

The other side suggests that responding to infant crying could actually increase the rate of infant crying, because the rate of crying essentially becomes strengthened or reinforced when responded to (Gewirtz & Boyd, 1977). This overall controversy seems central to the discussion about whether infants should be left to "cry it out" at any time.

In one study, St. James-Roberts et al. (2006) compared parents who held their infants a great deal of the time (on average 15 to 16 hours per day) versus those who held them much less. They found that the infants who were held much less cried 50% more overall.

Clearly the holding of infants is another important behavior that can reduce how stressed infants and their caregivers might be. This is supported by studies that show that infant crying is an important cause or at least precipitating event for abuse and maltreatment in a number of cases (Soltis, 2004).

Other Positive Socialization Benefits of Child-Centered Parenting

One of the additional benefits of child-centered parenting could be a closer sense of "connection" to other people. Because physical contact and touching is a less salient aspect of Western, and particularly Northern European cultures, this possible benefit has rarely been studied.

At the very least, parents who engage in highly responsive caregiving serve as models for their children. Thereby, they may promote higher frequencies of responsive, and even empathetic behavior toward others, as also noted by Bandura (1989).

Discussion and Conclusions

We have presented evidence that a number of child-centered practices may promote optimal development in a variety of ways. The discussion has focused primarily on practices that are related to soothing infants and reducing arousal, as these are most important, particularly during the early months, as far as buffering the infant against stressful events.

We have argued that reducing the number and kinds of early stressful events are important, having possible consequences both for the development of children's brains, and for their behavior. The argument is, that as seen in rodents and other mammals, the caregiver plays an important role, through his or her practices, in helping to tune or program the infant's stress-regulation system.

As infants continue to develop in many ways including attachment (Commons, 1991), their behavior and physiology changes. We have argued that the need for child-centered parenting does not end after the first few months of life, but that it continues, accommodating itself to developmental changes in young children (Miller & Commons, 2010).

To give one example, as children become more mobile, they will spend more time away from their parents and not being held. As research has also shown (e.g., Anderson, 1972), when the child initiates the departure from contact, and can rely on the parent remaining in the same location, they are more likely to freely explore.

When the parent initiates the separation, children have a great deal more trouble coping. In this case, children will be more likely to protest, and if possible to return to the parent's side (e.g., Ainsworth et al., 1978). Miller and Commons (2010) discuss several other possible changes in parenting behavior that might take place.

Parenting Behaviors that Cause Infant Stress Are Normative in the U.S.

It has to be noted that the types of parenting behaviors that might cause stress are considered by a large part of the population in the United States to be normative. As discussed by LeVine and colleagues (1994), by Richman, Miller, and Solomon (1988) and others, and these behaviors form part of a parenting strategy that emphasizes the infant and child's development of independence from the parent(s).

Parents who use these practices sincerely believe that it is most important to insist that the child behave independently, and that to "give in" to behaviors, such as crying or requests for attention, will simply encourage the child to become dependent. This belief is pervasive in this culture, so parents using "independence-promoting" strategies are, to a large extent, engaging in parenting that fits with the norms.

Individual Differences in Infants' Ability to Tolerate These Practices

Plus it would seem that some infants, and perhaps most, are able to tolerate these practices to some extent. So, some proportion of infants will learn—sooner or later—to fall asleep on their own. Many infants will eventually learn some self-consoling behaviors. As already noted, even though such infants may appear at that time to have mastered these tasks, one sometimes sees that the adaptation is not complete. For example, infants who have been sleeping alone often turn into toddlers and older children who seek comfort in their parents' bed when they are fearful or distressed.

129

We have also presented studies suggesting that the number of children using self-comfort objects, such as pacifiers, security blankets, or stuffed animals is much larger in the U.S. than in cultures in which infants and children neither sleep by themselves nor are encouraged to self-console (Miller & Commons, 2010).

Secondly, and as noted earlier, there are individual differences in how different infants may respond to the same kind of parenting practices, with some infants being more vulnerable than others. Some infants may seek physical contact more than others, and may not be at all easily consoled without it (Miller & Commons, 2010).

Some infants may be more easily consoled than others. Some infants may continue to sleep best with a parent or parents, whereas others may sleep well separately. The research on differential susceptibility that was cited earlier (Pluess & Belsky, 2009), as well as other studies (e.g., Caspi et al., 2002) have in fact confirmed that a "one size fits all" strategy will not work for every individual.

What Do Infants Learn from Independence-Promoting Strategies?

Even if an infant or child has largely coped with an independence-promoting strategy as opposed to one that is child-centered, as a culture we have to ask ourselves, what have they learned? Ultimately, they have learned that they are essentially alone. The lesson is repeatedly reinforced. If you are distressed, you must deal with it yourself. If you are frightened, don't bother us. The message is that there is "something wrong with you" if you are suffering too much.

Ultimately, this seems designed to not only reduce one's reliance on others, but can have the unintended consequence of our becoming completely alienated from those others. When we have what seems like an ever increasing incidence of lone and very lonely people perpetrating acts of violence against others, it might be that we should, as a culture, start asking the question as to whether the costs of our preferred childrearing strategies might be too high.

References

Ainsworth, M. D. S., Blehar, M. C., Waters, E., & Wall, S. (1978). *Patterns of attachment: A psychological study of the strange situation.* Hillsdale, N.J.: Erlbaum.

Anderson, J. W. (1972). Attachment behavior out of doors. In N. Blurton Jones (Ed.), *Ethological studies of child behavior* (pp. 199-215). Cambridge, U.K.: Cambridge University Press.

Bandura, A. (1989). Social cognitive theory. In R. Vasta (Ed.), *Annals of child development* (Vol. 6, pp. 1-60). Greenwich, CT: JAI Press.

Bell, S. M., & Ainsworth, M.D.S. (1972). Infant crying and maternal responsiveness. *Child Development, 43,* 1171-1190.

Caspi, A., McClay, J., Moffitt, T. E., Mill, J., Judy Martin, J., Craig, I. W., Taylor, A,, & Poulton, R. (2002). Role of genotype in the cycle of violence in maltreated children. *Science, 297*(5582), 851-854.

Commons, M. L. (1991). A comparison and synthesis of Kohlberg's Cognitive-Developmental and Gewirtz's Learning-Developmental Attachment Theories. In J. L. Gewirtz & W. M. Kurtines (Eds.), *Intersections with attachment* (pp. 257-291). Hillsdale, NJ: Erlbaum.

Gewirtz, J. L., & Boyd, E. F. (1977). Does maternal responding imply reduced infant crying? A critique of the 1972 Bell and Ainsworth report. *Child   Development, 48,* 1200-1207.

LeVine, R. A., Dixon, S., LeVine, S., Richman, A., Leiderman, P. H., Keefer, C. H., & Brazelton, T. B. (1994). *Child care and culture: Lessons from Africa.* New York: Cambridge University Press.

McKenna, J. J., & McDade, T. W. (2005). Why babies should never sleep alone: A review of the co-sleeping controversy in relation to SIDS, bedsharing, and breastfeeding. *Paediatric Respiratory Reviews, 6,* 134-152.

Miller, P.M., & Commons, M.L. (2010). The benefits of attachment parenting for infants and children: A behavioral developmental view. *Behavioral Development Bulletin, 10,* 1-14.

Pluess, M., & Belsky, J. (2009) Differential susceptibility to rearing experience: The case of childcare. *Journal of Child Psychology & Psychiatry, 50*(4), 396-404.

Richman, A., Miller, P., & Solomon, M. (1988). The socialization of infants in suburban Boston. In R. LeVine, P. Miller, & M. M. West (Eds.), *Parental behavior in diverse societies. New Directions in Child Development,* No. 40. San Francisco: Jossey-Bass.

Soltis, J. (2004). The signal functions of early infant crying. *Behavioral and Brain Sciences, 27,* 443-490.

St. James-Roberts, I. (2007) Helping parents to manage infant crying and sleeping: A review of the evidence and its implications for practice. *Child Abuse Review, 16*, 47-69.

Teti, D.M., Kim, B.-R., Mayer, G. & Countermine, M. (2010). Maternal emotional availability at bedtime predicts infant sleep quality, *Journal of Family Psychology, 24*(3), 307-315. doi: 10.1037/a0019306

Reprinted from *Clinical Lactation,* 2013, Vol. 4(2), 62-65. Used with permission.

Chapter 10

The Ethics of Early Life Care
The Harms of Sleep Training
Darcia Narvaez

Some argue that forcing babies into independent sleep-ing is good for them, increasing health and well-being. They argue that making babies learn to settle themselves at night helps them establish self-regulatory skills and makes them stronger. These practices are supposed to put babies on a road toward healthy physical outcomes, ensuring good sleep patterns. They are supposed to lead to emotional well-being, by ensuring children's ability to control themselves and establish self-reliance. These beliefs suggest that their advocates know very little about human development. It is a dangerous state of affairs.

What Do Babies Need and What Happens When We Ignore Those Needs?

Every animal has a developmental niche to promote optimal development in offspring. The niche represents a match between the needs of the offspring with environmental supports (i.e., parenting).

In comparison to other animal neonates, humans are still fetuses for nine to 18 months after birth. This means that for at least nine months postnatally their care should be as supportive and non-stressful as the womb. Because full-term infants are born with only 25% of the brain developed and many systems (e.g., immunity) are not fully functional for years, their early developmental niche is particularly influential, and is now known to affect long-term health and well-being (Shonkoff, 2012).

What Is Humanity's Evolved Developmental Niche?

Social mammals evolved a particularly intensive parenting style more than 30 million years ago, and until recently, humans have altered this only slightly. The components of the human evolved developmental niche (EDN) for early life include naturalistic birth (no separation of mother and baby, no induced pain or trauma), breastfeeding on demand for two to five years, nearly constant touch, responsiveness to the cues of the child, extensive positive social support including multiple adult caregivers, and free play with multi-aged mates.

Each of these factors is known to influence physical, mental, and psychosocial health. When the EDN is not followed, we can expect outcomes to be species atypical, not only in terms of health and well-being, but moral character (Narvaez, Panksepp, Schore, & Gleason, 2013; Narvaez, Wang, Gleason, Cheng, Lefever, & Deng, 2013).

If we turn to sleep training, we can see that it violates several characteristics of the EDN: (a) the infant is separated from adult bodies, which causes dysregulation of multiple systems; (b) breastfeeding on demand is made more difficult, depriving the child of the frequent bath of its hormones and body-building ingredients; (c) adults are, or are encouraged, to be too far away to be responsive, leading to distress and unanswered cues; and (d) the baby does not receive the social support it needs that builds a sense of self-confidence and trust. All told, the child's stress response, along with other systems, will be misdeveloped with long-term biopsychosocial-health effects.

Ethical Responsibilities

What Are the Ethical Obligations of Healthcare Providers to Babies?

The field of medicine has several ethical principles to which its practitioners typically subscribe. These include respect for a patient's autonomy, beneficence (acting in the best interest of a patient), promoting justice, and non-maleficence (do no harm) (Beauchamp & Childress, 2001). Let's take these four principles and apply them to infant care.

Autonomy

Children have little capacity for autonomy as infants. However, their autonomy as adults can be undermined if early care is not responsive to their needs. How is that possible? With undercare, they are less likely to develop secure attachment, with its accompanying neurobiology for sociality. They are less likely to be self-controlled and intelligent, at least in social and stressful situations (Narvaez, forthcoming; Narvaez, Gleason, Brooks, Wang, Lefever, Cheng, & Centers for the Prevention of Child Neglect, 2013).

Beneficence

Beneficence means that healthcare providers should be acting in the best interests of babies. To do this requires familiarity with the EDN and the effects of not following it (Narvaez, Panskepp et al., 2013). Violations of this principle occur when medical professionals do not follow the EDN. Advocating separation of caregiver and baby, sleep in isolation, crying it out, are all practices that violate the principle of beneficence.

Justice

Justice and fairness for whom? Doctors seem ready to put adults' needs first, minimizing needs of babies. The understanding of infant development and the EDN may improve attitudes toward providing for the baby's needs. The rights of babies need to be placed centrally in the eyes of healthcare providers and parents.

Non-Maleficence

From the viewpoint of the EDN, the principle of non-maleficence is being continually violated by current medical practices and directives. One assumes that these violations are due primarily to misinformation (i.e., a lack of knowledge of the EDN). But recent publications seem to intentionally mislead parents about what is good for babies.

Recently, the AAP's journal published a poorly wrought paper that claimed: "Behavioral sleep techniques have no marked long-lasting effects (positive or negative)" (Price et al., 2012). The authors drew this very strong conclusion even though they looked at only one and not all possible effects. Moreover, they did not examine what the control group families were doing, even though there are decades of studies on mammals showing the long-term harm that distressing young offspring can have on mammalian brains.

We know from animal studies, and from properly conducted human studies, that cry-it-out techniques harm babies. Even when sleep training is used, and the baby stops crying for help, this does not mean the baby is not stressed (though a parent may feel fine because the baby is not crying). Cortisol levels in the baby are still high, doing their damage to young neurons (Middlemiss et al., 2012).

1. **What does extensive distress do to a baby?** It can kill neurons, and misdevelop brain systems that undergird self-regulation, self-concept, and emotional intelligence. When children are under-cared for, that is, when they do not receive what they evolved to expect (i.e., the EDN), they are more likely to develop increased stress reactivity from poorly developed vagal tone (Porges, 2011), HPA axis (Lupien et al., 2009), and misdeveloped gene expression (Meaney, 2001, 2010).

2. **What does isolating infants do to them?** It causes multiple systems to become dysregulated, slowing down growth. Infants cannot self-calm, and so distress wreaks havoc on their development.

3. **What does encouraging parents to ignore signals from their infants do to the relationship?** It undermines parental sensitivity, one of the key

139

factors for optimal child development in every domain studied.

4. **What are the long-term effects of sleep training?** We do not know. Studies never examine all factors, and some are sloppy in determining what they are assessing in the control and experimental groups (see Middlemiss et al., in prep). But there are numerous animal studies with other mammals showing that even short-term separation from the mother can have long-term detrimental effects.

The great ignorance and disdain for babies shown by both the authors of the aforementioned study, and the editors of *Pediatrics,* is alarming. By allowing this irresponsible and unethical conclusion, the editors are encouraging parents to do great harm to their children and our fellow citizens. Such actions demonstrate deep cracks in professional ethical responsibilities.

How Can Healthcare Professionals Treat Babies Ethically?

The prism of ethics can be viewed in at least three ways: (a) following universal duties that anyone can carry out (i.e., the principles mentioned above), such as "do no harm"; (b) maximizing outcomes for all; and (c) taking virtuous action. We apply these approaches to the ethics of how adults (medical professionals and parents) might help babies sleep.

Do No Harm

The respect of persons often involves the principle of doing no harm (non-maleficence). Certainly we can agree that adults should try not to harm children. But then they require good information about what babies need. Babies need constant close contact with adults in early life. This suggests that healthcare providers ought to provide parents with alternatives to sleep training: ones that don't isolate babies from adult presence and touch.

Choose Actions that Result in the Best Outcomes for All Involved

A utilitarian approach attempts to maximize good outcomes for the greatest number of people. Certainly we need to be concerned for the needs of parents and supporting their well-being—exhausted parents are less able to take care of their children. However, babies have rights too. If you understand the EDN, you can see what rights babies should have, and how those rights are being violated routinely, even when there is no greater purpose for it.

Babies have the right to compassionate care from a welcoming community. They should not be subjected to painful experiences, such as cry-it-out techniques. They should not be isolated, untouched, or separated from the caregiver. Of course, they should receive the elixir of optimal development: breast milk. There are many other birthrights they should have too (see Narvaez , Panskepp et al., 2013).

Take Virtuous Action

Virtue involves behaving in the right way at the right time for the right reasons. Healthcare providers build their characters choice by choice. To be a virtuous professional means taking into account the whole context and one's impact in light of the type of professional one wants to be. The character of a community is also built choice by choice, action by action. To be a virtuous community means taking the welfare of all into account and lubricating everyone's path to virtue. For babies' sleep, this means helping parents find ways that work without creating difficulties for themselves or their babies.

Ethical Problem Solving

What are the best sleep solutions for all concerned? The most important aspect to work on may be to circumvent sleep problems in the first place.

Decrease Precursors to Sleep Problems

Of course, not having a sleep problem in the first place would be the best approach. Thus, a prevention focus may do the most good. This means we need to look at the precursors to why babies won't settle down and take care of those. What do we know about unsettled babies? We know that not meeting a baby's needs is very distressing—needs for touch, presence, and calming by parents.

There are other factors that lead to sleep disturbances, such as infant irritability and maternal distraction. Addressing these issues can head off potential sleep problems in infants.

1. Decrease stress on mothers during pregnancy (supporting moms with paid leaves from work and other support) (Davis et al., 2007).

2. Decrease stress on babies at birth by figuring out alternatives to practices that harm them and their ability to cope (e.g., some childbirth drugs undermine settling).

3. Establish on-demand breastfeeding immediately after birth.

4. Help parents learn to enjoy keeping their babies close and carrying them with movement.

5. Establish home routines for parents and babies early on that help babies sleep at night, such as exposure to light early in the day, and avoidance of light in the evening.

6. Provide regular home visits for new parents of nurse practitioners and lactation consultants to ensure responsive parenting is established.

All these practices require community support. The whole society must step in to support babies and their families.

Treat Babies with Equal Respect

I have sometimes wondered whether healthcare providers have forgotten about the welfare of babies beyond keeping them alive. Remember, that not too long ago women were treated like children by medical professionals (and still sometimes are). African Americans were treated as inferiors. It is time for healthcare providers to change their attitudes and treatment of babies.

They should:

1. Treat babies as equal human beings who cannot yet express themselves in words.

2. Respect the evolved developmental niche and preserve it.

3. Find ways that respect babies first, then parents.

Challenging Myths and Changing Culture

Why is it that there is such a strong focus and belief on the notion that early care should foster self-reliance and independence? And how did people come to believe that such early care leads to healthy children and strong societies? Why, when all these assumptions are completely wrong?

It's not just that healthcare providers have lost sight of what babies need; American culture has shifted away from providing the kinds of support babies need. Since at least the 19th century, mothers have been advised by experts to not "spoil" their children with too much attention. The mostly male experts argued that "coddling" children would make them weak and whiny, so it was best not to touch babies and children too much. A U.S. government pamphlet urged mothers not to be inconvenienced by babies, letting them sit silently in their beds (Ladd-Taylor, 1986). Interestingly, baby experts in Germany in the early 20th century (during the rise of the Nazis) advocated the same types of cold-heartedness toward babies (Chamberlain, 1997; Dill, 1999).

Sleep "experts" also emphasized parental detachment from the baby. Parents were to be in charge, not the baby. We can see where these practices have brought us. In the last 50 years, not only has EDN childrearing continued to decline, but child well-being in the USA has become among the worst in the developed world, with self-regulation, mental, and physical health continuing to deteriorate. Those under age 50 have a health disadvantage compared to those in 16 other developed countries (Institute of Medicine, 2013). The U.S. has epidemics of mental health problems in all ages in the country.

Humans are the most complex organism, with the most extensive maturational schedule. What happens early often lasts a lifetime (Shonkoff et al., 2012). Because of this all adults have an ethical responsibility to facilitate children's optimal development. The professionals with first contact of baby and mother may be the most important to lead the way to a cultural change of *putting babies first*.

References

Beauchamp, T. L., & Childress, J. F. (2001). *Principles of bio medical ethics.* New York: Oxford University Press.

Chamberlain, S. (1997). *Adolf Hitler, die deutsche Mutter und ihr erstes Kind. Über zwei NS-Erziehungsbücher. Giessen, Germany: Psychosozial-Verlag.* ISBN 3-930096-58-7.

Davis, E.P., Glynn, L.M., Dunkel-Schetter, C., Hobel, C., Chicz-DeMet, A., & Sandman, D.A. (2007). Prenatal exposure to maternal depression and cortisol influences infant temperament. *Journal of the American Academy of Child and Adolescent Psychiatry, 46*(6), 737-746.

Dill, G. (1999). *Nationalsozialistische Säuglingspflege.* Einefrühe Erziehung zum Massenmenschen. Stuttgart, Germany: Enke Verlag. ISBN 3 43230711 X.

Institute of Medicine. (2013). *U.S. health in international perspective: Shorter lives, poorer health.* Retrieved from: http://www.iom.edu/~/media/Files/Report%20Files/2013/US-Health-International-Perspective/USHealth_Intl_PerspectiveRB.pdf

Ladd-Taylor, M. (1986). *Raising a baby the government way: Mothers' letters to the Children's Bureau 1915-1932,* New Brunswick, NJ: Rutgers University Press.

Lupien, S.J., McEwen, B.S., Gunnar, M.R., & Heim, C. (2009). Effects of stress throughout the lifespan on the brain, behaviour and cognition, *Nature Reviews Neuroscience, 10*(6), 434-445.

Meaney, M.J. (2001). Maternal care, gene expression, and the transmission of individual differences in stress reactivity across generations. *Annual Review of Neuroscience, 24,* 1161-1192.

Meaney, M. (2010). Epigenetics and the biological definition of gene x environment interactions. *Child Development, 81*(1), 41-79.

Middlemiss, W., Granger, D.A., Goldberg, W.A., & Nathans, L. (2012). Asynchrony of mother–infant hypothalamic–pituitary–adrenal axis activity following extinction of infant crying responses induced during the transition to sleep. *Early Human Development, 88*(4), 227-232.

Narvaez, D. (forthcoming). *The neurobiology and development of human morality.* New York: W.W. Norton.

Narvaez, D., Gleason, T., Brooks, J. Wang, L., Lefever, J., Cheng, A., & Centers for the Prevention of Child Neglect (2013). *Longitudinal effects of ancestral parenting practices on early childhood outcomes.* Manuscript under review.

Narvaez, D., Panksepp, J., Schore, A., & Gleason, T. (Eds.) (2013). *Evolution, early experience and human development: From research to practice and policy.* New York: Oxford University Press.

Narvaez, D., Wang, L., Gleason, T., Cheng, A., Lefever, J., & Deng, L. (2013). The Evolved Developmental Niche and sociomoral outcomes in Chinese three-year-olds. *European Journal of Developmental Psychology.*

Porges, S. W. (2011). *The polyvagal theory: Neurophysiologial foundations of emotions, attachment, communication, and self-regulation.* New York: W.W. Norton.

Price, A.M.H., Wake, M., Ukoumunne, O.C., & Hiscock, H. (2012). Five-year follow-up of harms and benefits of behavioral infant sleep intervention: Randomized trial. *Pediatrics, 130*(4), 643 -651. doi: 10.1542/peds.2011-3467

Shonkoff, J.P., Garner, A.S., The Committee on Psychosocial Childhood, Adoption, and Dependent Care and Section on Developmental and Behavioral Pediatrics, Dobbins, M.I., Earls, M.F., McGuinn, L., ... & Wood, D.L. (2012). The lifelong effects of early childhood adversity and toxic stress. *Pediatrics, 129*, e232 (originally published online December 26, 2011).

Reprinted from *Clinical Lactation*, 2013, Vol. 4(2), 66-70. Used with permission.

Section III
Working with Parents Around
Sleep Issues

Chapter 11

Bringing the Parent Back into Decisions about Nighttime Care

Wendy Middlemiss

New parents often have many questions and concerns about how to help their children grow strong and healthy. Unfortunately, when it comes to nighttime care, healthcare providers often tell parents what to do rather than discussing options. Healthcare providers might give parents specific advice about how to handle nighttime wakings, for example, without inquiring about parents' beliefs and preferences. When healthcare providers simply tell parents what to do, parents may choose to ignore the advice if it is not consistent with their beliefs and preferences. When parents and healthcare providers do not communicate, parents do not get the information they need to cope with some of the more challenging aspects of infancy, including nighttime waking.

This chapter presents information on how to bring parents back into decisions about nighttime care by discussing issues more broadly, addressing parents' concerns regarding responsiveness, and focusing on the essentials of infant safety and health. When professionals can have open discussions with parents, parents gain the tools they need to make decisions that best fit their families' needs.

What Is the Allure of Reducing Nightwaking?

Healthcare providers often make specific recommendations about nighttime care that focus on reducing nightwakings, creating solitary sleep settings for infants, and limiting parents' contact with infants during their transitions to sleep. These recommendations for nighttime infant care reflect many common components of "best practice" recommendations (Morgenthaler et al., 2006) and American Academy of Pediatrics policy recommendations (American Academy of Pediatrics, 2000; 2011).

However, recommendations can sometimes limit conversation about developmentally appropriate sleep routines, infant safety, and flexibility in parent choices.

Of importance then, in supporting parents in their early care decisions, is to find a balance between the essential aspects of best-practice and policy recommendations, and parents' role in the decision making regarding care. With this, professionals can help parents create sleep routines that are safe, incorporate best-practice approaches, and fit the family's childrearing preferences.

Finding this balance can be very important when discussing issues, such as nighttime wakings and infants' ability to settle to sleep, without parents' assistance or presence. In this article, support for different sleep approaches is examined—with an eye toward facilitating discussions between parents and professionals.

Benefit or Risk?

Helping infants learn to sleep through the night without parents' help or attention is a compelling sleep goal. Controlled crying is one way that parents can achieve this end. Some healthcare providers like sleep-training approaches because they can be both simple to discuss, and successful, can result in fewer nightwakings requiring parent attention, and have outcomes that are easy to quantify.

Unfortunately, this successful approach does not take into account breastfeeding, parental responsiveness, normal fluctuations in infant sleep patterns at different ages, infant emotional regulation, maturity of infant autonomic functioning, infant settling and safety, or the parents' cultural preferences.

With this approach, infants can be "trained" to settle to sleep, and wake and resettle, without parental assistance through behavioral sleep interventions. Parents can be encouraged to focus on the goal of sleep consolidation. But is this an appropriate goal?

Certainly nightwakings, particularly in the context of helping infants settle to sleep, can be challenging for new parents. When infants wake, parents do too. This can influence parents' quality of sleep and their parenting efforts (McDaniel & Teti, 2013). Reducing nightwakings, then, benefits parents by increasing the duration of both

153

their sleep and their infants' sleep. Advocates of sleep training believe that the benefits of their approach clearly outweigh any potential costs (Price et al., 2012).

As noted in the previous section, however, the costs are far from negligible (see Miller & Commons and Narvaez, this volume). Infants can learn to settle themselves to sleep without parental assistance using behavioral-sleep interventions. However, even though infants stop crying for parents' attention, research has shown that infants continue to experience high levels of physiological distress (Middlemiss et al., 2012).

What this means is that infants appear to be able to settle to sleep without distress—which is very relieving for parents if their infants had been crying at nighttime. But infants are still experiencing distress even though they are no longer signaling that distress through crying. Considering that crying is an essential way for infants to communicate, the fact that they are no longer doing so is concerning.

This disconnect between infants' physiological experience of stress and their behavioral expression of this distress through crying is only one concern with behavioral approaches to nighttime care. There are other consequences when mothers are told to not respond to their babies' cries in order to eliminate nightwaking.

Non-responsive parenting may encourage mothers to establish routines that interfere with breastfeeding, and that do not support infants' biological and physiological development. Taken together as a whole, the cry-it-out approach gives mothers an inflexible set of baby-care rules that do not accommodate the normal fluctuations in breastfeeding, nightwakings, and infant growth.

Parents Become Less Comfortable Providing Infant Care

Thus, it is important to create discussions with parents that neither begin nor end with considerations of nightwakings. Childrearing is complicated, and there are many factors that contribute to its complexity. Mothers differ in their childcare preferences and the ease with which they transition to the role of caregiver.

In their recent study, Countermine and Teti (2010) examined a number of parenting factors, such as nighttime infant care, nightwakings, depression, and spousal agreement regarding infant care. They concluded that:

> The "best" sleep arrangements for infants may prove to be those that both parents are most comfortable with and that promote family harmony (p. 661).

Thus, rather than focusing on nightwakings—which is only one aspect of parenting—healthcare providers should help mothers find approaches that meet babies' needs and increase family well-being. Professionals can help parents make informed, comfortable choices about caring for their infants.

Is Comfort with Care That Important?

Recent research on parental adaptation, defined as parental comfort with their abilities as parents, suggests that parents are more effective when they are confident about their parenting skills (Countermine & Teti, 2010). Researchers have found that parents' comfort with

155

providing care is important in many different contexts. In looking specifically at infant nighttime care and adaptation, research indicates that when parents report high levels of stress, they have lower levels of parental self-efficacy (Jones & Prinz, 2005).

When the parents are responsive to infants' needs, parental adaptation predicts higher levels of functioning and adjustment in children over time (Countermine & Teti, 2010). In sum, parents who are well adapted, and have lower levels of parental stress, are more responsive during nighttime care, and report better quality of sleep (Ramos & Youngclarke, 2006). And when mothers are adapted, their babies sleep better too (Countermine & Teti, 2010).

Working with Parents to Develop a Strategy for Nighttime Care

Professionals can help parents construct a system of care that meets their infants' needs, and is appropriate for their caregiving preferences. Parents feel respected when professionals listen to their concerns. When the practices healthcare providers recommend are consistent with parents' values and beliefs, parents are more likely to incorporate these practices into their parenting (Nobile & Drotar, 2003).

Rather than simply focus on reducing nightwakings, you can work with parents to come up with strategies that address infants', mothers', and families' needs. You can incorporate their values into the nighttime-care plan, while encouraging parents to know their infants and trust their instincts for care. You can also help them be comfortable with different approaches to care and help them understand that their babies need them at night, and that parents also benefit when they are available to meet their infants' needs.

Below are some strategies for parents to help them cope with nighttime care and adapt to parenthood.

Know Your Infant, Trust Your Instincts

One of the first steps is helping parents understand the nature of nighttime care and infants' developing and fluctuating sleep patterns. Sharing this information with parents helps focus on identifying realistic expectations and helping parents understand what is essential to their infants, their caregiving, and their childrearing goals.

With this refocusing of discussions about infant sleep, parents can ask questions about nighttime care choices and related benefits or risks. For example, do parents want to sleep in the same bed and breastfeed their infant? If they do, then conversations can address the benefits of breastfeeding and infant safe-sleep environments, as well as likely sleep patterns.

Do parents want infants to sleep through the night? If so, discussion can include how to help parents address this goal without compromising breastfeeding or infants' natural need for responsiveness and proximity. With this focus, responsiveness and breastfeeding are not considered within the framework of infant nightwakings.

Nighttime wakings and crying become a natural and expected part of the sleep routine—one to be discussed, but not to be the central focus. When parents are comfortable with their care choices, and feel efficacious and well adapted to their role as parents, everyone in the family benefits (Middlemiss, 2010).

157

One benefit is lower likelihood of physiological distress at nighttime (Middlemiss, 2010). Infants receive care that builds their regulatory, social, and physiological systems and reflects their specific developmental needs.

Mothers can feel confident that they are meeting their infants' needs, while still tending to their own mental health (Thome & Skulladottirr, 2005), and cooperating with their partners in parenting decisions (McDaniels & Teti, 2013).

Comfort with Adapting Care to Your Infants' Changing Patterns

By refocusing conversations on a diversity of acceptable nighttime-care practices (i.e., not only practices that may reduce nightwakings), parents can become comfortable with adapting their care to their infants' needs. When mothers accept that there are different care choices, they are more likely to be adapted to their care choice.

This was demonstrated in a recent study of mothers. Mothers who chose to co-sleep still had higher stress levels when initiating the nighttime care than mothers whose babies slept alone. These findings were due, in part, to higher levels of stress associated with feelings of being criticized for their nighttime-care choices (Middlemiss et al., 2009).

The co-sleeping mothers were asked why they were satisfied with their decision to co-sleep, yet still reported high levels of stress. These mothers indicated that they were uncomfortable because they knew that co-sleeping was generally not accepted. Their personal comfort with the routine was compromised by the sense that they were not taking care of their infant the way that they "should," i.e., in a manner that limited parental presence and focused on nightwakings.

The mothers discussed, at length, their preferences for shared-sleep routines and the benefits they believed their infants derived from this type of care. Yet because they had heard that solitary sleep was the "best practice," they were uncomfortable with their care choice (Middlemiss et al., 2009).

Panchula (2012) discussed the importance of helping mothers be comfortable with their care routines. She noted that families' cultural framework is an important component of the type of care that the family will receive. In supporting families, it is essential to help them find solutions to problems that fit within the mothers' cultural preferences and their current situation. She emphasized that listening to parents is an important first step to any intervention.

With this approach, parents feel comfortable expressing their preferences, and professionals can provide guidance in a manner that resonates with parents' childrearing goals.

Helping parents feel comfortable with their childrearing choices is essential to successfully providing support and usable information (Ball et al., 2013; Cowan, 2012; Moon et al., 2008)—information that supports both continued breastfeeding and infant safety. Professionals can assure parents that nightwaking is often a normal sleep pattern for infants and toddlers.

Infants' sleep varies by how they are fed; whether parents are present while they sleep; and individual variables, such as temperament, prematurity, or well-being. All of these variables influence the nature and quality of infant sleep.

In their work, Thome and colleagues (2005) found that sharing information about normal infant sleep can have a positive impact on mothers' mental health.

Flexibility in Your Choices of Care

Mothers who wanted their infants to settle to sleep alone were less stressed when they were flexible with their care routines. In a study of infant sleep location, mothers who had firm beliefs about where babies should sleep were more stressed when they placed their infants in bed than mothers who were more flexible about sleep arrangements. Interestingly, this finding was true for both mothers who preferred that their infants sleep alone and mothers who believed they should be present while their infants slept (Yaure et al., 2011).

Mothers in both groups with flexible care routines (i.e., remaining with infants until they had fallen asleep and then placing them down) had lower levels of stress. This was even true for mothers who preferred that their infants have solitary, self-settling routines. This flexibility in routine can be helpful for parents as infants' patterns of sleep fluctuate with developmental changes, illnesses, and other factors.

With this flexibility, professionals are better positioned to help parents incorporate continued breastfeeding into their nighttime care choices—a choice that is ultimately of great benefit for both infant and mother.

Maternal flexibility has long-term effects. One of our studies explored the association between mothers' comfort with the sleep routine their five-year-olds had as infants, and their ratings of their children's social competencies. Mothers' comfort with their care practices was related to their children's social competency at age five years. Parental presence vs. self-settling was not (Middlemiss et al., 2002).

Sorting Out the Quandary of Remaining Present with Infants and Nightwakings

When professionals focus on how to best support breastfeeding and mother/infant sleep, they no longer need to focus solely on infant sleep location. This can help support parents in making choices that best fit their family and personal needs, as well as their infants' needs. For example, many parents prefer to be present during infants' nighttime routines, particularly as they transition to sleep (St. James-Roberts, 2007). This preference has been reported even for mothers focused on encouraging infant self-settling (Morgenthaler et al., 2006).

However, sometimes parents feel that they must choose between continued breastfeeding—often inclusive of nightwakings—or helping their infants learn self-settling routines. Self-soothing infants settle without parental assistance and sleep in locations portrayed to be the most safe.

If healthcare providers do not discuss benefits and risks of various sleep locations, parents may feel that the only two options are bedsharing or letting their babies cry in another room. To facilitate mothers' adaptation to care and comfort with their care choices, healthcare providers must share information regarding different approaches to nighttime care and their benefits for

161

families and infants. In the next section are some aspects of care that support choices across care routines.

Assurances of Infant Safety across Routines

Many parents prefer to remain with their infants during their transition to sleep, and many prefer to share sleep or bedshare. However, messages regarding the potential risk for infants in shared settings can lead parents to make choices that they do not feel comfortable with.

In making their decisions about nighttime care, parents may inadvertently introduce unnecessary risk in the nighttime routines. For example, proximity at night, although associated with more parental awareness of nightwakings, has been linked to an increase in response to infant distress, reducing infant stress reactivity, thus reducing this risk factor for future psychopathology (Tollenar et al., 2012).

Providing parents with information about safe infant sleep is critical. But such information needs to move beyond scare tactics and be more nuanced about what makes infant sleep healthy. It is important to assure parents that breastfeeding has been shown to reduce the risk of SIDS, particularly when bedsharing (AAP, 2011; McKenna, 2007).

Breastfeeding while bedsharing places infants in a safe position from which they are least likely to roll over to an unsafe position. A study examining mother and infant sleep environments found mothers engaged in different methods of protecting infants across different sleep settings (Volpe, Ball, & McKenna, 2013). Thus, discussions of safe infant sleep need to address different sleep practices.

When information about infant safety is not provided within the context of preference for care, infants' risks increase. Information is not heard as applicable to parents based on their choices for care (Moon et al., 2012).

The essentials of infant sleep are not discussed and parents often are left to ignore both the essential components of care protective of infants and the components of care that do not fit within their family system. Because infant safety can be assured across a diversity of sleep settings, sharing information about parents' preferred care routine is essential.

Understanding the Value of Responsiveness and Presence

Part of the quandary regarding nighttime care comes from the general sense that being present during nighttime care harms infants and keeps them from developing healthy sleep routines. Parents are particularly concerned that being present for their infants will lead to more nightwakings and poorer infant sleep. It is important, then, to assure parents that responsiveness is essential and help parents incorporate responsiveness within their preferred sleep routines. This may be the first step to helping parents establish and maintain breastfeeding across nighttime care.

Perceiving cries as needing attention has been found to be an important factor in mothers' response (Middlemiss et al., 2009). Mothers least likely to perceive infants' cries as needing attention were less likely to attend to infants. This lack of response, however, was

163

associated with infants experiencing higher levels of physiological stress during their transition to sleep in comparison to infants whose mothers perceived their cries as indicating distress.

The value of responsiveness moves beyond that of its developmentally appropriate nature in supporting infants' development. Parents who respond to their infants' cries have higher levels of adaptation to parenting during nighttime care (Teti et al., 2010), and greater parental efficacy in comparison to parents who did not respond to their babies and practiced sleep training and other parental-sleep routines (Countermine & Teti, 2010).

When parents ignored their babies' cries as a means of reducing nightwakings, it was problematic for parents and infants (France & Blampied, 2005; Morgenthaler et al., 2006). Not responding to infants' cries also led to higher levels of infant stress (Yaure et al., 2011). Telling parents about the benefits of responsive parenting can help them feel good about their parenting choices and/or help them be flexible in their nighttime parenting approaches.

Summary and Conclusions

What does this research on infant-sleep practices mean, then, for practice? Perhaps of greatest import is the message that mothers' comfort with and adaptation to the role of care provider is essential to helping families transition to parenting.

By talking to parents about nighttime care practices in general, rather than focusing only on nightwakings, lactation consultants become guides who both share information with parents and gather information from them. In helping mothers establish early-care routines, you can actually support mothers, rather than "supporting" them by focusing on infants sleeping through the night, scheduled feedings, and other means of controlling a routine or schedule.

These interventions, even when successful in the short term, may have high costs. You can support mothers by helping them understand the importance of knowing and having a relationship with their infants, and how to balance infant care with providing for their own needs. With a broader focus on normal infant sleep behavior, and realistic expectations for early care, parents can have a clearer understanding, and be more knowledgeable and accepting as they establish healthy and appropriate care routines.

Parents often anticipate that the "terrible twos" — whether terrible or not so bad — will be a time of toddlers proving that they are "able to do it by themselves." Adolescence can be a time of conflict between parents and teens. So it follows that infancy can be a time marked by nightwakings, and that responsiveness is important to meeting these care needs. Thus, in working with new parents, it is important to help them understand that there are many times infants will wake, and that there are many options for care.

What may be most helpful is to let parents know that early nighttime care can be a challenging time, when parents are tired and sometimes frustrated or flustered. Discuss with parents what to expect, and how they can meet their babies' needs. This can provide parents with the assurance that they can find "their" best way to parent.

The role of the professional is essential in providing parents with the tools to establish their routines, to meet the changes and challenges, and to be comfortable with how their care will provide a strong foundation for their child's developing emotional wellbeing, physical well-being, and brain.

References

American Academy of Pediatrics Task Force on Infant Sleep Position and Sudden Infant Death (2000). Changing concepts of sudden infant death syndrome: Implications for infant sleeping environment and sleep position. *Pediatrics, 105,* 650-656.

American Academy of Pediatrics, & Task Force on Sudden Infant Death Syndrome. (2011). Policy Statement: SIDS and other sleep-related deaths: Expansion of recommendations for a safe infant sleeping environment. *Pediatrics, 128*(5), 1030-1039.

Ball, H.L., & Volpe, L. (2013), Sudden Infant Death Syndrome (SIDS) risk reduction and infant sleep location—Moving the discussion forward. *Social Science & Medicine, 79,* 84-91.

Countermine, M.S.. & Teti, D.M. (2010). Sleep arrangements and maternal adaptation in infancy. *Infant Mental Health Journal, 31*(6), 647–663. DOI: 10.1002/imhj.20276

Cowan, S. (2012). Creating change: How knowledge translates into action for protecting babies from Sudden Infant Death? *Current Pediatric Reviews, 6,* 86-94.

McDaniel, D. T., & Teti D. M. (2013). Coparenting quality during the first three months after birth: The role of infant sleep quality. *Journal of Family Psychology, 26,* 886-895.

McKenna, J. J., Mosko, S. S., & Richard, C. A. (1997) Bedsharing promotes breastfeeding. *Pediatrics, 100,* 214–219.

Meijer, A.M. (2011). Infant sleep consolidation: New perspectives. *Sleep Medicine Reviews, 15,* 209–210. doi:10.1016/j.smrv.2011.01.004

Middlemiss, W., Granger, D.A., Goldberg, W.A., & Nathans, L. (2012). Asynchrony of mother–infant hypothalamic–pituitary–adrenal axis activity following extinction of infant responses induced during the transition to sleep. *Early Human Development, 88,* 227-232. doi:10.1016/j. earlhumdev.2011.08.010

Middlemiss, W. (2010, August). *Working with families through a process orientation: Focusing on best practices through family strengths.* Invited paper presented at the International Scholar Series at Ewha Woman's University, Seoul, Korea.

Middlemiss, W. (2005). Prevention and intervention: Using resiliency-based multisetting approaches and a process-orientation. *Child and Adolescent Social Work Journal, 22,* 85-103.

Middlemiss, W. (2004a). Infant sleep: A review of normative and problematic sleep and interventions. *Early Child Development and Care, 174*(1), 99-122. doi:10.1080/0300443032000153516

Middlemiss, W. (2004b) Work in progress: Defining problematic infant sleep: Shifting the focus from deviance to difference. *Zero to Three, 24,* 46-51.

Moon, R. Y., Calabrese, T., & Aird, L. (2008). Reducing the risk of Sudden Infant Death Syndrome in child care and changing provider practices: Lessons learned from a demonstration project. *Pediatrics, 122,* 788-798.

Nobile, C., & Drotar, D. (2003). Research on the quality of parent-provider communication in pediatric care: Implications and recommendations. *Journal of Developmental & Behavioral Pediatrics, 24*(4), 279-290.

Panchula, J. (2012). Working with families of different cultures I. Lessons learned. *Clinical Lactation, 3*(1), 13-15.

Price, A.M.H, Wake, M.,Ukoumunne, O.C., & Hiscock, H. (2012). Outcomes at six years of age for children with infant sleep problems: Longitudinal community-based study. *Sleep Medicine, 13,* 991-998. doi: 10.1016/j.sleep.2012.04.014

Sadeh, A., Tikotsky, L., Scher, A. (2010). Parenting and infant sleep. *Sleep Medicine Review, 14,* 89-96

St. James-Roberts, I. (2007). Infant crying and sleeping: Helping parents to prevent and manage problems. *Sleep Medicine Clinics, 2*(3), 363-375, DOI: 10.1016/j.jsmc.2007.05.015.

Teti, D.M., & Crosby, B. (2012). Maternal depressive symptoms, dysfunctional cognitions, and infant night waking: The role of maternal nighttime behavior. *Child Development, 83,* 939–953. DOI: 10.1111/j.1467-8624.2012.01760.x

Teti, D.M., Kim, B.-R., Mayer, G., & Countermine, M. (2010). Maternal emotional availability at bedtime predicts infant sleep quality. *Journal of Family Psychology, 24*(3), 307-315. doi: 10.1037/a0019306

Thome, M., & Skulladottir, A. (2005). Evaluating a family-centered intervention of infant sleep problems. *Journal of Advanced Nursing, 50,* 5-11.

Volpe, L. E., Ball, H. L., & McKenna, J. J. (2013). Nighttime parenting strategies and sleep-related risks to infants. *Social Science & Medicine, 79,* 92-100.

Yaure, R., Middlemiss, W., & Huey, E. (2011, November). *Infant nighttime care: What should we consider?* Paper presented at the National Council on Family Relations Annual Conference, Orlando, FL.

Reprinted from *Clinical Lactation,* 2013, Vol. 4(2), 71-76. Used with permission.

Chapter 12

Is Your Baby's Sleep a Problem? Or Is It Just Normal?

Tracy Cassels
Sarah Ockwell-Smith
Wendy Middlemiss
Kathleen Kendall-Tackett
Helen Stevens
Darcia Narvaez

Most new parents complain about lack of sleep. Many are also concerned that their babies have a "sleep problem," and that what they are experiencing isn't "normal." So they search books, ask friends and family—or even their doctor—what they should do about their child's problematic sleep patterns. And they worry about it—a lot.

Part of this epidemic of parental angst about children's sleep is that we live in a culture in which parents are repeatedly told that they *need* to worry about their child's sleep, that there will be dire consequences if their child doesn't get enough sleep. Another problem is that most new parents, having had little experience with children prior to having their own, have little awareness about what truly is "normal" when it comes to infant sleep.

Simply being made aware of normal sleep patterns can help alleviate the stress and anxiety parents feel, leading to happier times for the entire family.

So What Is Normal?

This paper describes some of the more common sleep concerns parents have with the hope that they can see them as normal, developmental stages for their child.

Waking through the night is normal and biologically adaptive.

The Critical Roles of Feeding Method and Changes in Development

"My child wakes every hour, all day and night, to feed."

Whether it's every hour, or every two hours, or even three, parents are often concerned when their young infant is waking regularly for feedings. This concern is not surprising given the focus on "sleeping through the night" that our culture pushes. But sleeping through the night is not biologically normal, especially for a breastfeeding baby.

At the time of birth, a baby's stomach can only hold a teaspoonful worth of milk, meaning that he or she will need to feed frequently to meet the many demands for energy that accompany this period of growth. Although the stomach grows relatively quickly, the fat and protein content in human breast milk is much lower than in the milk of other mammals, and thus infants are required to feed often, resulting in greater night wakings (Ball, 2003; Ball, 2009).

Human milk, being designed for infants who need to feed on cue day *and* night, is easily and quickly digested. Formula, however, is typically made from the milk of another species–cows–and is higher in fat while also containing myriad additives that make it more difficult, and thus slower, to digest. This can affect infant sleep, resulting in unnaturally deeper infant sleep (more time spent in stage 3-4; Butte, Jensen, Moon, Glaze, & Frost Jr., 1992). Stage 3-4 is most difficult to arouse from to terminate breathing pauses. This is especially true for infants who are arousal deficient. Longer stages of Stage 3-4 sleep could potentially diminish the infant's capacity to maintain sufficient oxygen. Even so, formula use does not necessarily provide parents with more sleep overall (Doan, Gardiner, Gay, & Lee, 2007; Kendall-Tackett, Cong, & Hale, 2011).

Infants whose primary source of energy is breast milk will often wake frequently to nurse, something that is essential for the breastfeeding relationship to continue (Ball, 2009). However, regardless of feeding status, many infants wake regularly during the night (Weinraub, Bender, Friedman, Susman, Knoke, Bradley, et al., 2012). *Waking through the night is normal and biologically adaptive.* In fact, though it is often reported that sleep patterns consolidate in the second year, the pattern differs in breastfed children.

Breastfeeding mothers may wake more often, but report greater total sleep time. For example, in a study of 6,410 mothers of infants 0 to 12 months old, exclusively breastfeeding mothers reported both more wakings and more total sleep time compared with mixed- or exclusively formula-feeding mothers (Kendall-Tackett, Cong, & Hale, 2011, this volume). The exclusively breastfeeding mothers reported less daytime fatigue, more energy, less anger and irritability, and lower levels of depressive symptoms.

Interestingly, mothers who were both breast and formula-feeding reported fewer hours of sleep than exclusively breastfeeding mothers, *and there was no significant difference between the mixed- and formula-feeding mothers on any of the outcome measures* (Kendall-Tackett, Cong, & Hale, 2011, this volume). This is important because new mothers are often pushed to supplement to "get more rest." These results, consistent with the findings of Doan et al. (2007), suggest that *supplementing actually results in less sleep — not more.*

Night wakings continue to be common as breastfeeding infants mature. In a study of children who were breastfeeding at age two, night wakings were common throughout the second year of life. This pattern of night wakings is commonly observed in cultures where co-sleeping and full-term (aka, "extended") breastfeeding are more common (Elias, Nicolson, Bora, & Johnston, 1986).

Night Wakings Protect Infants

Night wakings have been reported as being more common in infants who bedshare with a parent, yet the wakings and bedsharing (when done safely) may actually protect infants from SIDS (Mosko, Richard, & McKenna, 1997; Mosko, Richard, McKenna, & Drummond, 1996). The critical period for SIDS is up to eight months of age (with the peak at two to three months), and night wakings may serve as a protective mechanism. In fact, if we look at parenting historically and cross-culturally, frequent night wakings, coupled with co-sleeping and breastfeeding, are the norm for which we should be comparing other infant sleep behaviors.

"My child was sleeping through the night and suddenly stopped."

Imagine you've been waking regularly with night feeds and arousals, but as time passes they are decreasing. Then you realize you're now sleeping in nice, long chunks. Hours of sleep all at once! And it's wonderful. Then suddenly, as quickly as it came, it's gone. Your wonderful, sleeping-through-the-night child is suddenly waking again. This experience, which is a reality for many, can cause frustration and despair accompanied by the feeling that you've done something wrong, or that you must do something to get their uninterrupted sleep back again.

Here's the thing: You didn't *do* anything. *A return to night waking after periods of sleeping through the night is entirely normal.* Many children's sleep will cycle like this for a while. In fact, researchers looking at sleep patterns have found that often between 6 and 12 months, infants who had previously been sleeping long stretches suddenly start to wake more frequently at night (Scher, 1991, 2001). In one long-term study looking at child sleep between three and 42 months found that there was *no* stability in night wakings, or even sleep duration, during this time (Scher, Epstein, & Tirosh, 2004).

What Causes the Change in Sleeping Pattern?

There are likely a variety of reasons, unique to each child. For some, it may be a growth spurt or teething. For others, it may be a cognitive leap that has them buzzing more so than usual or the appearance of separation anxiety. Just recently a study reported that babies tend to wake more often when they are learning to crawl. And for some, we may never know the actual reason. But as children age, and each develops a circadian rhythm, they will go through cycles of sleep– some more convenient for parents than others.

Parents need to be aware that these changes are entirely normal, even though they can be frustrating. Hopefully, once you know that changes are to be expected, you can be better prepared, or at least not add anxiety to the sleep disruptions you are forced to deal with once again.

"My child wakes up at 2 a.m., and is up for one to two hours!"

One mother remembers very clearly the first time her daughter ended up doing this. At around 14 months, she woke up in the middle of the night and didn't seem ready or able to go back to sleep for one to two hours no matter what strategies her parents tried. This continued regularly for a couple of months. And then as quickly as it started, it stopped, and hasn't happened again in over a year.

If bedsharing works for a family, no one should tell them to stop.

The "why" of this is relatively unknown—although researchers are continuing to explore the physiological underlyings of sleep—but we do know that extended night wakings like these are experienced by many children until around three years of age (Weinraub, Bender, Friedman, Susman, Knoke, Bradley et al., 2012). *Many times the wakings are brief and the child settles quickly. Other times settling takes longer. In either case, these wakings do not suggest your child has a sleep "problem."*

Increased night wakings, call-outs, and crying are more common around six months of age or so, and again as infants near two years of age. *These wakings may simply be one (of many) manifestations of separation anxiety experienced by the child*—a normal change resulting from infants learning that they exist separately from their caregivers (for a review, see Middlemiss, 2004).

Some argue that night wakings in toddlerhood are reflective of sleep problems, but these opinions are based on criteria that do not necessarily reflect the realities of infant sleep. Several studies found that night waking is relatively common between age 12 and 24 months (Richman, 1981; Goodlin-Jones, Burnham, Gaylor, & Anders 2001; Scher, 2000; Weinraub et al., 2013).

Thus, a parent's perceptions about what constitutes a sleep problem may be triggered by either a disconnect between expectations of uninterrupted sleep and a toddler sleep pattern that arguably falls within the range of normal, or by the impact that night waking has on the parent's quality of sleep and daily functioning (Loutzenhiser, Ahlquist, & Hoffman 2012). However, although changes in sleep patterns may be inconvenient and frustrating, they are normal occurrences in the context of a healthy parent-child relationship.

When viewed as indicating problematic, rather than normal sleep patterns that will come and go, parents can experience greater stress and worry (Middlemiss, 2004). As we have learned from many parents, understanding that these night wakings are normal can go a long way toward making them more bearable.

The Importance of Understanding Individual Patterns in Sleep

"My child won't go to sleep before 10 p.m."

It is not uncommon in some parts of Western societies to assume that infants and young children must be in bed by, for example, 7 p.m. to develop "good sleep habits." *Unfortunately, that's just not the reality for many families, and it's not because parents are negligent in getting their infants to bed, but because some children simply have a different circadian rhythm, or a later schedule may work for the family.* Some children will continue this pattern into their toddler years and beyond.

Cross-cultural data on bedtimes for infants and toddlers shows that later bedtimes are actually quite frequent in predominantly Asian countries (Mindell, Sadeh, Wiegand, How, & Goh, 2010). Whereas the mean bedtime for children in predominantly Caucasian countries was found to be 8:42 p.m, it was a full hour later for predominantly Asian countries (with a mean at 9:44 p.m.), with the latest mean bedtime being 10:17 p.m. in Hong Kong. Notably, the rising time was also significantly later in these countries. A concurrent finding was that the vast majority of children in predominantly Asian countries sleep either in the parent's bed or room. *Thus, children who sleep with their parents may naturally have a sleep schedule closer to their parents owing to the sleeping arrangements.*

What is important to remember is that a late bedtime, in and of itself, is not a problem. If it poses a problem for the family as a whole, then parents may want to adjust the bedtime routine (Mindell, Telofski, Weigand, & Kurtz, 2009), or start the routine earlier in small increments in order to gradually move to an earlier bedtime (Richman, 1981).

"My child sleeps less than (or more than) the recommended amount no matter what I do!"

Most people have seen the "sleep guidelines" about how much sleep our children need at various stages. Parents are told that newborns should sleep around 16 to 18 hours, that at two years of age, children require a total of 13 hours sleep, and so on. *When researchers explore questions of how long infants and children should sleep, and what are healthy recommendations, the answers are not particularly clear,* and are often based on examining how much children *are sleeping* at different times in history (Matricciani, Olds, Blunden, Rigney, & Williams, 2012).

As parents, it is important to remember that these are *recommendations.* Each child is different, and the recommendations may not fit every child. Some will require much more sleep, and some will require less. *If a child is truly sleep deprived, there will be noticeable signs.* Signs of sleep deprivation include rubbing eyes, looking dazed, and not focusing on people or toys, becoming overly active late at night, and having a hard time waking up in the morning.

By paying attention to your child's cues and behaviors, you will be able to tell if your child is getting enough sleep, regardless of the exact number of hours he or she sleeps. Sleep is important, but there are many ways to get it apart from one long, uninterrupted stretch.*

Interestingly, researchers are now telling us that waking in the middle of the night is common in adulthood and was viewed as normal in past eras—the "first sleep" lasted about four hours, with an awake period in between, followed by a "second sleep" of another four hours (for more details, *At Day's Close: Night in Times Past* by Roger Ekirch: Norton, 2005).

Normal Parent Behaviors and Why They Won't Hurt Your Child

"My child is still sleeping in our bed."

Many parents who sleep with their child get comments along the lines of, "Your child will never leave if you don't move them" or "What about your sex life?" Parents end up questioning if they are doing the right thing for their children, or if they will end up with a 16-year-old who still wants to crawl into bed with mom and dad every night. First, let's address the question of when a child leaves the bed. Rest assured that your child will not be dragging you off to college so they can still sleep with you--*even if you don't force them out of the bed.*

The age at which children are ready to move into their own room varies widely, and bedsharing is quite common worldwide. Notably, bedsharing rates in Scandinavian and Asian countries are much higher than those in the U.S. or Canada (Mindell, Sadeh, Wiegand, How, & Goh, 2010; Nelson & Taylor, 2001; Welles-Nystrom, 2005; for a review, see Cassels, 2013). Parents polled by one of the authors about the age at which their children initiated the move to another room report ages as young as 18 months, and as old as 10 years.

Some factors that influence the transition age include: having a sibling in the other room (thus being able to room-share with another child), the presence of a new baby in the bed (and needed attention to safety for the new baby and disrupted sleep for the older child), and the child's own developmental needs. Each family will need to consider the factors that are relevant for their particular child.

181

The research on extended bedsharing has not found any social, emotional, or cognitive detriment for bedsharing children relative to children who were placed in their own room in infancy (e.g., Abel, Park, Tipene-Leach, Finau, & Lennan, 2001; Barajas, Martin, Brooks-Gunn, & Hale, 2011; Keller & Goldberg, 2004; Okami, Weisner, & Olmstead, 2002).

The second issue that is often brought up has to do with the marital relationship when the family bed is utilized. New research looking at bedsharing and marital satisfaction has reported *no influence of bedsharing on the marital relationship when bedsharing is intentional* (Messmer, Miller, & Yu, 2012). When bedsharing is in reaction to child sleep problems, parents may report greater stress on their relationship, but it is likely that this is due to the problems associated with infant sleep problems. As to intimacy, parents of co-sleepers and bedsharers often find creative ways to make sure their needs are met as well. There are excellent (and humorous) blogs on the topic if you're in need of some extra assistance.

"My child only goes to sleep breastfeeding."

Most parents in the early months know how quickly an infant can go to sleep while breastfeeding. In fact, breastfeeding often is what sends our little ones to sleep. Although many people do not think twice about these behaviors when their infants are still quite tiny, they start to worry about it as the child ages. It doesn't help that "falling to sleep" while breastfeeding is listed as one of the sleep disorders by sleep researchers (Melzer & Mindell, 2006), and that often family and friends will tell you that you're harming your child, and that he or she will "never" learn to fall asleep on his or her own. Many "sleep experts" will recommend not letting your infant fall asleep on your breast for fear of creating this "bad habit" (Meltzer & Mindell, 2006), instead recommending that you rouse your little one before putting him or her down.

If you don't have a problem with breastfeeding your child until they are sleeping, and placing them down while sleeping, you don't need to worry about it for your child. How can we say this? First, a child who is tired enough will fall asleep with or without breastfeeding. Although falling asleep at the breast may remain a *preferred* way to fall asleep for a child (full of the closeness and intimacy that is so necessary for bonding), it will not be a necessary step.

As children age, they will fall asleep in various places and positions. *Young infants should not be forced to fall asleep without comfort; they may need to breastfeed to feel relaxed and safe enough to enter sleep.* Another factor to remember is that *all children eventually wean.* Breastfeeding and cuddling to sleep offer comfort for your child, a closeness that is associated with positive developmental outcomes. Children will seek this closeness as a natural part of development. This is not a bad thing; it is simply offering your child the closeness that is a natural part of growth and parenting.

If still uncertain, *be assured that breastfeeding is a natural way to help children sleep and provide important support for their growth.* Parents should know that breast milk in the evening contains more tryptophan (a sleep-inducing amino acid). Tryptophan is a precursor to serotonin, a vital hormone for brain function and development. In early life, tryptophan ingestion leads to more serotonin receptor development (Hibberd, Brooke, Carter, Haug, & Harzer, 1981).

Nighttime breast milk also has amino acids that promote serotonin synthesis (Delgado, 2006; Goldman, 1983; Lien, 2003). Serotonin makes the brain work better, keeps one in a good mood, and helps with sleep-wake cycles (Somer, 2009). So because of tryptophan and its wider effects, it *may be especially important for children to have evening or night breast milk for reasons beyond getting them to sleep.*

The other concern that is brought up is that infants and children who fall asleep at the breast (or even in-arms) often wake looking for the same environment in which they first fell asleep (Anders, Halpern, & Hua, 1992). This can lead to crying upon waking when they find themselves in a different environment, such as a crib.

For parents who bedshare and breastfeed, parents have reported decreased signaling as infants learn to seek mother's breast and latch themselves on to breastfeed when waking at night. *Though arousals continue to be greater in bedsharing dyads* (Mosko, Richard, & McKenna, 1997), *this natural interaction provides a soothing and simple way to care for infants as they wake.* In these cases, when the children are developmentally ready, putting them down nearly asleep, and letting them finish the process on their own, may help reduce wakings that result in signaling for the parent.

"My child only naps when I'm outside/walking/ on me."

Wouldn't it be nice if infants and children wanted to sleep exactly where we wanted to put them on a given day? No joke here–it would be wonderful, but unfortunately it's not how most babies sleep. We've heard of mothers complaining about having to be outside walking for a nap to happen while living in cities with blizzards and 30 below weather, or needing to be walking constantly (inside or out), meaning naps are not only not a time of respite for mom, but can be downright unpleasant.

Interestingly, the most common situations involve touch, sound, or movement--three things that are abundant for the infant while in the womb. Recall that human babies are born at least nine months early compared to other animals because of head size (if they got any bigger they could not get through the birth canal; see Trevathan, 2011), so for at least nine months their bodies expect an "external womb."

So is it much of a surprise that outside the womb they expect the same things to lull them to sleep? With respect to **touch,** we know that oxytocin plays a huge role in feelings of contentment, security, and love, all of which affect the quality of our sleep (Uvnäs-Moberg,

Parents should not expect their infants (or toddlers) to sleep through the night as they have myriad needs that require parental responses, even during the night.

2003). So it is not difficult to imagine that infants who are physically close to their caregivers, experiencing a release of oxytocin, are much more likely to fall asleep and remain asleep.

A second factor is **sound**–most notably the caregiver's heartbeat, a sound that is highly familiar to infants from their time in the womb. When it is the mother holding the infant, her heartbeat, voice, and breathing can all offer a form of white noise, which helps an infant feel safe and remain asleep, though the same effects can happen when another caregiver holds the infant as well.

When this is not possible, the use of a white noise machine to block out some of the more abrasive sounds of our environment while still providing background noise can help with infant sleep. These white noise machines have been successful in inducing infant sleep (Spencer, Moran, Lee, & Talbert, 1990), and at assisting some parents achieve better sleep (Lee & Gay, 2011).

The third factor, **movement**, was also abundant in the womb, with baby in a soft, liquid pouch being swayed regularly. Remember how your baby was always awake in utero when you were resting? It's because he or she was sleeping while you moved. Modern parents in Western cultures often focus on the car ride to get their infants to sleep. The lull of the car coupled with the snugness of the car seat can send many infants into a drowsy state, allowing them to nap contently while parents drive aimlessly around.

However, the same movement-induced sleep can be gained from the use of a stroller, providing mom or dad with the ability to run errands, or go for a walk or run. Possibly best of all, babywearing promotes movement, touch, and sound, all while allowing the caregiver to run errands, and generally go about one's life. Babywearing may provide the best form of an "external womb" for developing the baby's brain and body in optimal ways (Narvaez et al., 2013).

The take-home point, though, is *that it is normal for infants to prefer to sleep in contact with others rather than away from what many people would consider the "ideal" sleep space.* Even though adults may prefer it, a bed in a quiet room is not necessarily ideal for infant naps.

A Final Summary

We hope we have made it clear that often what parents perceive to be problematic infant sleep patterns that require "fixing" are actually quite normal and developmentally appropriate. We are cognizant of the fact that many families still find infant and toddler sleep to be a problem, which is why we are also focusing on writing about how to gently help with infant and toddler sleep.

What we hope parents take home from this series is (a) a better understanding of the broad array of behaviors that constitute "normal" when it comes to our children's sleep, and (b) that if the behaviour is not posing a problem for the family, you can rest assured the child is not suffering from these very normal sleep behaviors. Instead of following a particular expert's advice, understand what is needed to keep babies safe when they sleep and build the sleep environment around these safe behaviors. Then do what works best for your child.

Let your child be your guide.

References

Anders, T.F., Halpern, L.F., & Hua, J. (1992). Sleeping through the night: A developmental perspective. *Pediatrics, 90,* 554-560.

Ball, H. L. (2003). Breastfeeding, bed-sharing, and infant sleep. *Birth, 30,* 181-188.

Ball, H. L. (2009). Bed-sharing and co-sleeping: Research overview. *NCT New Digest, 48,* 22-27.

Barajas, R.G., Martin, A., Brooks-Gunn, J., & Hale, L. (2011). Mother-child bed-sharing in toddlerhood and cognitive and behavioral outcomes. *Pediatrics, 128,* e339-e347.

Butte, N. F., Jensen, C. L., Moon, J. K., Glaze, D. G., & Frost Jr., J. D. (1992). Sleep organization and energy expenditure of breast-fed and formula-fed infants. *Pediatric   Research, 32,* 514-519.

Cassels, T.G. (2013). ADHD, sleep problems, and bed sharing: Future considerations. *The American Journal of Family Therapy, 41,* 13-25.

Delgado, P.L. (2006). Monoamine depletion studies: Implications for antidepressant discontinuation syndrome. *Journal of Clinical Psychiatry, 67*(4), 22-26.

Doan, T., Gardiner, A., Gay, C. L., & Lee, K. A. (2007). Breast-feeding increases sleep duration of new parents. *Journal of Perinatal & Neonatal Nursing, 21,* 200-206.

Elias, M. F., Nicolson, N. A., Bora, C., & Johnston, J. (1986). Sleep/wake patterns of breast-fed infants in the first 2 years of life. *Pediatrics, 77,* 322-329.

Goldman, A. S. (1993). The immune system of human milk: Antimicrobial anti-inflammatory and immunomodulating properties. *Pediatric Infectious Disease Journal, 12*(8), 664-671.

Goodlin-Jones, B. L., Burnham, M. M., Gaylor, E. E., & Anders, T. F. (2001). Night waking, sleep-wake organization, and self-soothing in the first year of life. *Journal of   Developmental and Behavioral Pediatrics, 22*(4), 226.

Hibberd, C.M., Brooke, O.G., Carter, N.D., Haug, M., & Harzer, G. (1981). Variation in the composition of breast milk during the first five weeks of lactation: implications for the feeding of preterm infants. *Archives of Diseases of Childhood, 57,* 658-662.

Kendall-Tackett, K. A., Cong, Z., & Hale, T. W. (2011). The effect of feeding method on sleep duration, maternal well-being, and postpartum depression. *Clinical Lactation, 2*(2), 22-26.

Lee, K.A. & Gay, C.L. (2011). Can modifications to the bedroom environment improve the sleep of new parents? Two randomized control trials. *Research in Nursing and Health, 34,* 7-19.

Lien, E.L. (2003). Infant formulas with increased concentrations of α-lactalbumin. *American Journal of Clinical Nutrition, 77*(6), 1555S-1558S.

Loutzenhiser, L., Ahlquist, A., & Hoffman, J. (2011). Infant and maternal factors associated with maternal perceptions of infant sleep problems. *Journal of Reproductive and Infant Psychology, 29*(5), 460-471.

Matricciani, L. A., Olds, T. S., Blunden, S., Rigney, G., & Williams, M. T. (2012). Never enough sleep: A brief history of sleep recommendations for children. *Pediatrics, 129*, 548-556.

Meltzer, L.J., & Mindell, J.A. (2006). Sleep and sleep disorders in children and adolescents. *Psychiatric Clinics of North America, 29*, 1059-1076.

Messmer, R., Miller, L.D., & Yu, C.M. (2012). The relationship between parent-infant bed sharing and marital satisfaction for mothers of infants. *Family Relations, 61*, 798-810.

Middlemiss, W. (2004). Infant sleep: A review of normative and problematic sleep and interventions. *Early Child Development and Care, 174*, 99-122.

Mindell, J. A., Sadeh, A., Wiegand, B., How, T. H., & Goh, D. Y. T. (2010). Cross-cultural differences in infant and toddler sleep. *Sleep Medicine, 11*, 274-280.

Mindell, J. A., Telofski, L. S., Weigand, B., & Kurtz, E. S. (2009). A nightly bedtime routine: Impact on sleep in young children and maternal mood. *Sleep, 32*, 599-606.

Mosko, S., Richard, C., & McKenna, J. (1997). Infant arousals during mother-infant bed sharing: Implications for infant sleep and sudden infant death syndrome. *Pediatrics, 100,* 841-849.

Mosko, S., Richard, C., McKenna, J., & Drummond, S. (1996). Infant sleep architecture during bedsharing and possible implications for SIDS. *Sleep, 19,* 677-684.

Narvaez, D., Panksepp, J., Schore, A., & Gleason, T. (Eds.) (2013). *Evolution, early experience and human development: From research to practice and policy.* New York: Oxford University Press.

Nelson, E.A.S., & Taylor, B.J. (2001). International child care practices study: infant sleeping environment. *Early Human Development, 62,* 43-55.

Richman, N. (1981a). A community survey of characteristics of one to two-year-olds with sleep disruptions. *Journal of the American Academy of Child Psychiatry, 20,* 281-291.

Richman, N. (1981b). Sleep problems in young children. *Archives of Disease in Childhood, 56,* 491-493.

Scher, A. (1991). A longitudinal study of night waking in the first year. *Child: Care, Health and Development, 17,* 295-302.

Scher, A. (2001). Attachment and sleep: A study of night-waking in 12-month-old infants. *Developmental Psychobiology, 38,* 274-285.

Scher, A., Epstein, R., & Tirosh, E. (2004). Stability and changes in sleep regulation: A longitudinal study from 3 months to 3 years. *International Journal of Behavioral Development, 28,* 268-274.

Somer, E. (2009). *Eat your way to happiness.* New York: Harlequin.

Spencer, J.A., Moran, D.J., Lee, A., & Talbert, D. (1990). White noise and sleep induction. *Archives of Diseases in Childhood, 65,* 135-137.

Trevathan, W.R. (2011). *Human birth: An evolutionary perspective.* New York: Aldine de Gruyter.

Uvnäs-Moberg, K. (2003). *The oxytocin factor: Tapping the hormone of calm, love and healing.* Cambridge, MA: Da Capo Press.

Weinraub, M., Bender, R. H., Friedman, S. L., Susman, E. J., Knoke, B., Bradley, R., Houts, R., & Williams, J. (2012). Patterns of developmental change in infants' nighttime sleep awakenings from 6 through 36 months of age. *Developmental Psychology, 48,* 1511-1528.

Welles-Nystrom, B. (2005). Co-sleeping as a window into Swedish culture: considerations of gender and health care. *Scandinavian Journal of Caring Science, 19,* 354-360.

Reprinted from a Praeclarus Press White Paper: *Is Your Baby's Sleep a Problem? Or Is It Just Normal?* This paper is available for free download from Praeclarus Press (www. PraeclarusPress.com). Used with permission.

Chapter 13

We Go Together Like... Breastfeeding and Cosleeping

Tracy Cassels

"100 years of rapidly changing infant-care fashions cannot alter several million years of evolutionarily derived infant physiology"

—Helen Ball

Sleep and feeding have become two of the most discussed and disseminated topics in parenting today. How much sleep are you getting? Do you use formula or just the breast? When should a child sleep through the night? Do you pump? Does dad feed the little one at all? Do you room-share, bedshare, or put the little one alone in his room? What about sex?

There is an endless array of questions and judgments and "shoulds" associated with both infant sleep and feeding. But this hasn't always been the case. It used to be a simple matter of mother breastfeeding, and mother and infant sleeping together with no judgment and no questions about quality or quantity of sleep. For this reason, breastfeeding and co-sleeping are huge parts of evolutionary parenting; they facilitate the bond between mother and infant via skin-to-skin contact (Uvnas-Moberg, 2003), co-sleeping works to keep baby's temperature and breathing regulated (Ball, Blair, & Ward-Platt, 2004; McKenna & McDade, 2005), and it seems to provide parents and baby with better sleep (McKenna, Ball, & Gettler, 2007), while breastfeeding offers vital immune protection to infants necessary for survival (Duijts, Jaddoe, Hofman, & Moll, 2010).

Where Babies Sleep and How They Feed

For most mothers in contemporary Western societies, breastfeeding and infant sleeping arrangements are two distinct parenting practices with little or no relation to one another. To talk about one is not to talk about the other. Biologically, however, the two are inextricably intertwined.

For much of human history, Hunter-Gatherer societies dominated and in this domain, women were as central to the survival of the clan as men. There were no maternity leaves, but the work done by women was of the less-dangerous gatherer type, meaning they were able to do their work with children and infants in tow.

But with this came the necessity for women to sleep well, as a woman who is sleep-deprived does not serve anyone well in any capacity (it is truly strange that we have adopted the modern view that sleep deprivation is a "normal" state of affairs with a newborn).

As for the infant, without any alternatives, they required their mother's breast milk to survive, much less thrive. And thus we reach the point at which breastfeeding and cosleeping collide — in order to breastfeed continuously without immense sleep interruption mothers must cosleep; and on the flipside, cosleeping allows mothers to breastfeed more often, providing more nutrition for a developing infant.

Biologically, our bodies have evolved to both breastfeed and cosleep, and each seems to have helped facilitate the other. So how did this separation occur, and what does it mean for infant well-being and parenting practices in Western societies?

There seem to be distinct reasons for the reduction in breastfeeding and cosleeping in Western societies, yet they obviously affect each other. With respect to breastfeeding, we see the rise of the industrial society, which sent women to work, and science with all its might creating formula, which was believed to be superior to breast milk by doctors for quite some time.

These two factors alone had a huge impact on reducing breastfeeding rates in Western societies. This reduction of breastfeeding meant that sleeping arrangements were also free to change. But in addition, there was an even greater impetus for change – the belief in fostering independence.

Sleep Location and Babies' Independence

The juxtaposition of a baby's dependence/ interconnectedness and independence/autonomy has dictated parenting practices around the world, though not always in the same manner. For example, in America the newborn is viewed as entirely dependent upon its mother.

Yet the desired end-goal is for that baby to be an independent and autonomous individual. Thus, our practices are geared towards that end-goal; we put babies alone in their own room, we don't touch them very often, and we've even removed the dependence on mother for breastfeeding through the use of formula.

In contrast, the Japanese view the newborn as an autonomous, independent being who must be held, breastfed, and touched regularly (cosleeping is the norm there), in order to build the feelings of interconnectedness they value (Caudill & Weinstein, 1969). Similarly, research from New Zealand has found that cultural groups that share the Western-independence view rarely sleep with their infants, while Pacific cultural groups demonstrate lots of sleep contact because they believe that interconnectedness is the way to foster a child's development (Abel, Park, Tipene-Leach, D., Finau, S., & Lennan, M., 2001).

So while there are myriad factors why any one individual would choose to cosleep or not, or breastfeed or not, culturally this notion of independence has played a very large role in shaping our collective views on the issue.

The problem for Western cultures is that the Western assumptions of what fosters independence seem to be, well, wrong. Research has demonstrated that the Eastern interconnectedness model fosters independence and well-being to a much greater degree than simply forcing children to try and be independent.

One such example is the case of the Sami and Norwegian children. Sami individuals are more likely to cosleep with their children, and their children were found to be more independent and demand less attention from their parents than Norwegian children, who typically sleep alone (Arnestad, Andersen, Vege, & Rognum, 2001).

Interestingly, thanks to a push to increase breastfeeding rates in Norway, cosleeping has also become a more common sleeping arrangement (Arnestad et al., 2001), and children are reaping the benefits. Similar relationships have also been found in Sweden, where breastfed infants were much more likely to sleep with their parents than formula-fed infants (Lindgren, Thompson, Haggblom, & Milerad, 1998).

The Logistical Benefits of Bedsharing

I have mentioned some of the logistical reasons for breastfeeding and cosleeping to go together, but is there more than that? After all, if it's a matter of pure logistics, wouldn't it simply be a matter of whatever works to separate the two? Turns out there are a couple of rather important effects that each practice has on the other. Let's start with the effects of cosleeping on breastfeeding. As previously mentioned, cosleeping rates are greater amongst breastfeeding mothers (Blair & Ball, 2004), and while increasing breastfeeding has increased cosleeping rates (Arnestad et al., 2001; Lindgren et al., 1998), the fact is that cosleeping actually *facilitates* more breastfeeding. If you compare mothers who breastfeed, those who cosleep breastfeed up to twice as much at night over those who do not (McKenna, Mosko, & Richard, 1997; See also Ball, this volume).

Why is this important? Dr. Helen Ball has done research on the effects of sleep location on breastfeeding and come to some interesting (though expected) conclusions. Namely, cosleeping right from the start reduces the chances of having breastfeeding problems. Specifically, Dr. Ball looked at sleep locations for new mothers and their infants, and randomly assigned women to one of three location types – either those that facilitated mother-infant access (i.e., bedsharing or putting the infant in a three-sided crib that was attached to the parent bed, much like an official Co-Sleeper), or those that did not (i.e., a stand-alone bassinette next to the mother's bed).

Bedsharing Increases Nighttime Suckling

Mother-infant dyads that had sleeping arrangements that facilitated mother-infant access showed greater successful suckling than those who were in the stand-alone bassinette group (Ball, 2006a). Upon follow-up with these mothers, Dr. Ball found that these effects of early cosleeping continued at 16 weeks, with twice as many mothers in the unhindered-access groups both breastfeeding, and exclusively breastfeeding (Ball & Klingaman, 2007).

This study does not even consider infants in a separate room, as all three groups were room-sharing. But it was the bedsharing (or three-sided crib) that facilitated breastfeeding. Why does this happen? As previously mentioned, infants who cosleep tend to feed (or at least suckle) for twice the amount of time as non-cosleeping infants (Blair & Ball, 2004).

Stimulation of the nipple is necessary for the production of prolactin, the hormone that allows for milk secretion. Thus the reduction in suckling can lead to deleterious effects on milk production or the maintenance of a mother's milk supply (Neville, Morton,& Umemura,

2001). In short, when mothers get their babies into bed with them right away, they reduce the chances of having low milk production when breastfeeding.

Now, what of the effects of breastfeeding on bedsharing? First, you must remember that the biggest argument against bedsharing has to do with infant deaths. Many people argue that bedsharing increases the risk of death via suffocation or SIDS. While there is no direct evidence that breastfeeding *causes* a reduction in SIDS *for bedsharing babies*, there is ample circumstantial evidence to suggest this is the case.

Bedsharing and Breastfeeding Lowers Risk of SIDS

Most prominently, cross-cultural data shows that cultures in which bedsharing *and* breastfeeding are the norm have substantially lower SIDS rates than cultures in which they are not the norm (Lee, Chan, Davies, Lau, & Yip, 1989; Nelson & Taylor, 2001; Watanabe, Yotsukura, Kadoi, Yashiro, Sakanoue, & Nishida, 1994).

For example, Japan has long been considered the pinnacle of success with respect to SIDS deaths, as their rates are generally half of other industrialized nations, and bedsharing is also the norm there. It is possible that breastfeeding has nothing to do with their lower SIDS rates, except that we know breastfed babies are at a much lower risk for SIDS more generally (Ford, Taylor, Mitchell, Enright, Stewart, Becroft, & Scragg, 1993; Fredrickson, Sorenson, Biddle, 1993; Hoffman, Damus, Hillman, & Krongrad, 1988; Ip, Chung, Raman, Chew, Magula, DeVine, Trikalinos, & Lau, 2007; Mitchell, Taylor, Ford, Stewart, Becroft, Thompson, Scragg, Hassall, Barry, & Allen, 1992).

Breastfeeding in and of itself reduces the risk of SIDS. In a meta-analysis on the relationship between breastfeeding and SIDS, researchers found that while any breastfeeding more than halves the risk of SIDS, exclusive breastfeeding has an ever greater effect (Hauck, Thompson, Tanabe, Moon, & Vennemann, 2011). Furthermore, duration and intensity of breastfeeding have also been found to relate to SIDS levels, with greater duration and intensity leading to a lower risk of SIDS (McKenna & McDade, 2005).

Bedsharing babies breastfeed up to twice as long as non-cosleeping babies. It is, therefore, not unreasonable to assume that the extra breastfeeding during cosleeping further increases protection against SIDS.

Breastfeeding and Bedsharing Can Prevent Infant Failure to Rouse

An additional hypothesis for how breastfeeding may reduce the risk of SIDS for cosleeping infants comes from Dr. James McKenna, who has posited that the arousals from breastfeeding keep the infant from falling into a deeper sleep, which may lead to a "failure to rouse" (Mosko, Richard, & McKenna, 1997). This "failure to rouse" has been discussed as a potential mechanism behind SIDS; infants reach too deep a level of sleep and they are simply incapable of coming out of it, similar to entering a coma.

Breastfeeding, thus, increases the number of infant arousals (though not full wakings), and this is greater during cosleeping, and is especially true for breastfeeding dyads not only because of mother's movements, but because of the frequency of feedings.

Breastfeeding and Infant Sleep Position

Another way in which breastfeeding may help reduce the risk of SIDS is by influencing the position in which the infant sleeps. Breastfeeding infants are less likely to sleep prone because it doesn't facilitate breastfeeding; in order for an infant to breastfeed, he or she needs to be on his or her back or side. An infant in the prone position simply cannot reach or latch onto the breast (unless the prone position is on mother). Infant position also helps reduce the chances of infants suffocating, as a baby in the prone position who cannot roll over, is at greater risk for suffocation.

Breastfeeding Impacts Mothers' Sleep Behaviors

Breastfeeding also seems to be related to practices that reduce the risk for suffocation. Research has found that maternal-infant behavior during sleep is different for mothers who breastfeed compared to mothers who formula feed (Ball, 2006b). Behaviors, such as facing the infant and having the infant lie at chest level, being much more prominent in breastfeeding dyads. These behaviors may seem trivial, but they can be imperative for keeping an infant safe.

For example, a child who lies at chest level (as opposed to head level, which is what Dr. Ball found to be more common in formula-fed infants who coslept) is less likely to be surrounded by pillows, which increases the risk for suffocation. They are also less likely to be too close to a headboard, which is another known hazard. Babies have fallen between the headboard and mattress, and suffocated.

There is also more eye contact between mother and baby during a breastfeeding session than during a bottle-feeding session (Else-Quest, Hyde, & Clark, 2003). Bonding that occurs during daytime feedings may serve to heighten the mother's awareness of her baby, leading her to be intuitively safer at night. That is, a mother who has bonded with her child is more aware of her child's presence at any given point. This has not been formally studied. But it is plausible that the security of attachment between mother and baby may also protect babies while they sleep.

The Benefits of Bedsharing and Breastfeeding

Hopefully, the link between breastfeeding and cosleeping is now clear. The benefits they offer each other are neither superfluous nor easily available by other means. In changing our parenting practices, we have developed other problems. Western countries have alarmingly high rates of breastfeeding problems, and much higher rates of infant mortality (notably SIDS), than other countries who have similar medical advancements, but also breastfeed and bedshare on a regular basis.

Interestingly, we also have a high rate of sleeplessness by new mothers—so much so that we joke about never sleeping again when people have a new baby—and our children have unusually strong attachments to objects for sleep (e.g., security blankets, stuffed animals). Neither of these is universal. In fact, research has shown that breastfeeding mothers who cosleep get more sleep than both bottle-feeding mothers and mothers who breastfeed, but do not bedshare (Quillin & Glenn, 2003, see also Kendall-Tackett, Cong, & Hale, 2011, this volume).

Additionally, children who are solitary sleepers show a greater need and use for security objects and sleep aids (Hayes, Roberts, & Stowe, 1996). So not only do our sleep and feeding practices have significant consequences (i.e., breastfeeding troubles and infant death), we see smaller consequences in the majority of new mothers and their children. Isn't it time we recognized not only the benefits of bedsharing and breastfeeding, but the symbiotic nature of the two?

References

Abel, S., Park, J., Tipene-Leach, D., Finau, S., & Lenan, M. (2001). Infant care practices in New Zealand: A cross-cultural qualitative study. *Social Science & Medicine, 53,* 1135–1148.

Arnestad, M., Andersen, M., Vege, A., & Rognum, T.O. (2001). Changes in the epidemiological pattern of sudden infant death syndrome in southeast Norway, 1984–1998: Implications for future prevention and research. *Archives of Diseases of Childhood, 85,* 180–185.

Ball, HL. (2006a). Bed-sharing on the post-natal ward: Breastfeeding and infant sleep safety. *Journal of the Canadian Paediatric Society, 11,* 43A–46A.

Ball, H.L. (2006b). Parent-infant bed-sharing behavior: Effects of feeding type, and presence of father. *Human Nature, 17,* 301–316.

Ball, H.L., Blair, P.S., & Ward-Platt, M.P. (2004). "New" practice of bedsharing and risk of SIDS. *The Lancet, 363,* 1558.

Ball, H.L., & Klingaman, K.P. (2007). Breastfeeding and mother-infant sleep proximity: Implications for infant care. In: W. Trevathan, E.O. Smith EO, & J.J. McKenna (Eds.) *Evolutionary medicine, 2nd Ed* (226-241). New York: Oxford University Press.

Blair, P.S., & Ball, H.L. (2004). The prevalence and characteristics associated with parent-infant bed-sharing in England. *Archives of Diseases of Childhood, 89*, 1106-1110.

Caudill, W., & Weinstein, H. (1969). Maternal care and infant behaviour in Japan and America. *Psychiatry, 32*, 12–43.

Duijts, L., Jaddoe, V.W.V., Hofman, A., & Moll, H.A. (2010). Prolonged and exclusive breastfeeding reduces the risk of infectious diseases in infancy. *Pediatrics, 126*, e18-e25.

Else-Quest, N.M., Hyde, J.S., & Clark, R. (2003). Breastfeeding, bonding, and the mother-infant relationship. *Merrill-Palmer Quarterly, 49*, 495-517.

Ford, R.P., Taylor, B.J., Mitchell, E.A., Enright, H.W., Stewart, A.W., Becroft, D.M., & Scragg, R. (1993). Breastfeeding and the risk of sudden infant death syndrome. *International Journal of Epidemiology, 22*, 885–890.

Fredrickson, D.D., Sorenson, J.F., & Biddle, A.K. (1993). Relationship of sudden infant death syndrome to breast-feeding duration and intensity. *American Journal of Diseases of Children, 147*, 460.

Hauck, F.R., Thompson, J.M.D., Tanabe, K.O., Moon, R.Y., & Vennemann, M.M. (2011). Breastfeeding and risk of sudden infant death syndrome: A meta-analysis. *Pediatrics, 128*, 1-10.

Hayes, M.J., Roberts, S.M., & Stowe, R. (1996). Early childhood co-sleeping: Parent-child and parent-infant nighttime interactions. *Infant Mental Health Journal, 17*, 348-357.

Hoffman, H., Damus, K., Hillman, L., & Krongrad, E. (1988). Risk factors for SIDS: Results of the institutes of child health and human development SIDS cooperative epidemiological study. In P. Schwartz, D. Southall, & M. Valdes-Dapena (Eds.), *Sudden infant death syndrome: Cardiac and respiratory mechanisms* (Annals of the New York Academy of Science). New York: National Academy of Sciences.

Ip, S., Chung, M., Raman, G., Chew, P., Magula, N., DeVine, D., Trikalinos, T., & Lau, J. (2007). *Breastfeeding and maternal and infant health outcomes in developed countries*. Evidence report/technology assessment number 153. Agency for Healthcare Research and Quality, Rockville, MD (2007). http://www.ahrq.gov/clinic/tp/brfouttp.htm

Lee, N.Y., Chan, Y.F., Davies, D.P., Lau, E., & Yip, D.C.P. (1989). Sudden infant death syndrome in Hong Kong: Confirmation of low incidence. *British Medical Journal, 298,* 721.

Lindgren, C., Thompson, J.M.D., Haggblom, L., & Milerad, J. (1998). Sleeping position, breastfeeding, bedsharing and passive smoking in 3-month-old Swedish infants. *Acta Paediatrica, 87,* 1028–1032.

McKenna, J.J., Ball, H.L., & Gettler, L.T. (2007). Mother-infant co-sleeping, breastfeeding and sudden infant death syndrome: What biological anthropology has discovered about normal infant sleep and pediatric sleep medicine. *Yearbook of Physical Anthropology, 50,* 133-161.

McKenna, J.J., & McDade, T. (2005). Why babies should never sleep alone: A review of the co-sleeping controversy in relation to SIDS, bedsharing and breast feeding. *Paediatric Respiratory Reviews, 6,* 134-152.

McKenna, J.J., Mosko, S., & Richard, C. (1997). Bedsharing promotes breast feeding. *Pediatrics, 100,* 214–219.

Mitchell, E.A., Taylor, B.J., Ford, R.P.K., Stewart, A.W., Becroft, D.M., Thompson, J.W., Scragg, R., Hassall, I.B., Barry, D.M., & Allen, E.M. (1992). Four modifiable and other major risk factors for cot death: The New Zealand study. *Journal of Paediatric & Child Health, Suppl 1*, S3–S8.

Mosko, S., Richard, C., & McKenna, J.J. (1997). Infant arousals during mother-infant bed sharing: Implications for infant sleep and sudden infant death syndrome research. *Pediatrics, 100*, 841-849.

Nelson, E.A.S., & Taylor, B.J. (2001). International child care practices study: Infant sleeping environment. *Early Human Development, 62*, 43–55.

Neville, M.C., Morton, J., & Umemura, S. (2001). Lactogenesis: The transition from pregnancy to lactation. *Pediatric Clinics of North America, 48*, 35-52.

Quillin, S.I.M., & Glenn, L.L. (2003). Interaction between feeding method and co-sleeping on maternal-newborn sleep. *Journal of Gynecology and Neonatal Nursing, 33*, 580-588.

Uvnas-Moberg, K. (2003). *The oxytocin factor: Tapping the hormone of calm, love, and healing.* Cambridge, MA: Da Capo Press.

Watanabe, N., Yotsukura, M., Kado,i N., Yashiro, K., Sakanoue, M., & Nishida, H. (1994). Epidemiology of sudden infant death syndrome in Japan. *Acta Paediatrica Japan, 36*, 329–332.

Reprinted from Evolutionary Parenting, http:// evolutionaryparenting.com/we-go-together-like-breastfeeding-and-co-sleeping/, posted July 19, 2011. Used with permission.

Chapter 14

Simple Ways to Calm a Crying Baby
And Have a More Peaceful Night's Sleep

Sarah Ockwell-Smith
Darcia Narvaez
Wendy Middlemiss
John Hoffman
Helen Stevens
James McKenna
Kathleen Kendall-Tackett
Tracy Cassels

"My baby is only happy in my arms. The minute I put her down she cries."

"She wakes every hour throughout the night, every night. I'm exhausted."

Most Infants Wake at Night and Expect Comfort from their Parents

The number of times infants wake and need help to return to sleep decreases as they grow, but still remains fairly common. Recent research by Weinraub and her colleagues confirms how *normal it is for babies to wake at night*, with 66% of 6-month-olds still waking at least once or twice a week, and the remaining babies waking even more often. Some babies will cry when waking at 12 months of age—even babies who have settled back to sleep on other nights.

Helping an infant return to sleep easily, then, is an essential gift to give our infants, and an important goal for parents who need to rest. The science of nighttime care provides a good foundation for parents trying to calm their babies. It clarifies what is important to know about calming babies, and why certain types of calming are most likely to be helpful.

What Is Important to Know about Calming

A parent's presence helps to calm babies who awaken in an upset state

Babies (especially in the first few months) are not yet capable of regulating their emotional states. This is one of the reasons why crying tends to increase in the first two to three months of life, and then decrease steadily after that. Infants cry or fuss for many reasons, including hunger, pain, or other discomforts or, at times, simply a desire for physical contact. For example, infant crying/

fussing behavior generally decreases by as much as 43% at six weeks of age (Hunziker & Barr, 1988).

Fussing and crying are the most important means by which an infant communicates needs and desires. The specific reason cannot always be determined, but for sure, displaying visible and audible signs of distress is an infant's most important defense and is overwhelmingly adaptive. When upset, babies depend on sensory input from caregivers—touch, soothing voice, smell, eye gaze, breastfeeding—in order to calm down. That's the way nature designed it to work.

Babies rely on their caregivers to calm them and to help deal with other reasons they are unhappy or uncomfortable, such as being in pain, hungry, or in some sort of physical or emotional state that we can't determine. Being present and attending to infants when they wake and cry can help infants return to sleep more quickly (Mao, Burnham, Goodlin-Jones, Gaylor, & Anders, 2004).

Calming infants helps infants learn to calm themselves

By helping infants calm down by attending to their distress, caregivers help infants develop the tools—both physiologically and emotionally—to calm themselves. This is what parents help children with generally (Davidov & Grusec, 2006; Stifter & Spinrad, 2002). Parents are often hesitant to be present when babies cry, fearing that attending to crying babies will lead babies to be unable to deal with distress on their own. But this approach only leads to a fussy baby and a clingy child.

Leaving babies to cry increases babies' stress levels and often keeps them awake longer. It does not guide them emotionally or physically toward the goal of regulating their own distress and response. Instead, to develop "good" or "healthy" sleep habits, gentle parental guidance is needed to resettle. Over time this leads to a strong, self-settling child who can calm him or herself when challenges arise.

Bottom Line

Crying upon waking is a perfectly normal behavior. Helping crying infants feel comforted and calm supports their developing abilities to calm themselves over time.

Understand why some babies fuss more at night than other babies

Fussing upon awakening is a perfectly normal behavior. When babies are distressed they are indicating a need for attention, often to help them recover a feeling of security. It is, however, important to understand that babies differ in what makes them feel secure.

Because some infants don't cry very much or very forcefully, some people develop the expectation that all babies can/should be like that. But babies vary greatly in terms of how often and how hard they cry. These differences are driven by many factors, including temperament, experience and physiological maturity. Thus, the need for external regulation (calming) continues in varying degrees for different babies.

Providing external regulation for babies who feel less secure, and thus more distressed, actually *helps* them, not hinders them. It helps them build the neural pathways that eventually enable them to deal with stress and calm themselves (Cassidy, 1994; Stifter & Spinrad, 2002).

Understand when waking is a problem

Waking is a normal part of infant sleep, and varies based on several infant factors: (a) feeding method (breast or bottle), (b) age, (c) shifts in developmental levels, and (d) individual level of maturity. In light of these factors, every family must determine whether an infants' waking is a problem for the family. Waking isn't a problem just because it happens. To suggest waking defines "problematic sleep" does not accurately reflect current science.

We know that it is normal for infants to wake several times in the night, especially if breastfeeding. And given that human babies are neurologically immature at birth, awakenings are the infants' major line of defense against dangerous, prolonged breathing pauses and permits oxygenation. Moreover, transient and more prolonged awakenings can help respond to cardiopulmonary challenges while asleep and restore a more natural heart rhythmicity (Mosko et al., 1997a).

Recall that the early research on sudden infant death syndrome (SIDS) revealed that infants who woke frequently in the night were less likely to die of SIDS than those who awakened significantly less often (see review in McKenna 1995 and Mosko et al., 1997a and b).

Even then it may be more helpful to frame the night waking as a family problem rather than as a child's "sleep problem." If a parent is OK with a baby waking two or more times a night at 12 months then there is no problem!

After babies are beyond the age of chief risk for SIDS and their waking and sleeping is settling into more of a consistent pattern, research shows that many continue to wake in the night (Weinraub et al., 2012).

Calming Ways to Calm Babies

The first three months of life is known to many as "The Fourth Trimester" and requires similar care to the womb. Some babies make the womb-to-world transition easily, others less so. Many of the ways parents naturally try to calm babies actually re-create many of the comforting, familiar experiences infants had during their time in utero. For all babies, these calming techniques can be very comforting.

Parents can help recreate these calming environments across any sleep routine and sleep pattern. It's important to remember what is calming and why.

Recreate movement

The womb is a constantly moving space and babies tend to respond by calming to movements, such as dancing, swaying from side to side, going for an exaggerated quick walk, or bumpy car ride.

Rely on touch; Provide skin-to-skin contact

Being in contact with warm, naturally (un)scented, skin is proved to be calming for infants/babies, it helps to stabilize their body temperature, heart rate, and stress hormones, and stimulates the release of oxytocin—the love and bonding hormone–in parent and baby both.

Recreate familiar sounds

The babies' time in the womb was marked by many rhythmic sounds. Sounds similar to those babies heard in the womb can be very calming. White noise offers constant surrounding sounds while also slowing brain wave frequencies.

Help the infant learn to deal with sensations of hunger

Hunger is a new sensation for infants—and infants may find it hard to calm when they feel hungry. Feeding babies when they wake at night can help babies transition back to sleep, especially when lighting and interaction are kept at low levels of stimulation.

Babies also find sucking to be the ultimate relaxation and comfort tool, one of their few forms of self-initiated self-regulation. Sucking helps a baby's skull bones to return to their normal position after birth as well as providing them with comfort and security. Some infants/babies respond to sucking on a dummy/ pacifier as soothing (but avoid this in the early weeks of breastfeeding as it can pose problems establishing breastfeeding). Non-nutritive suckling on the breast is also calming.

Parents can help recreate these calming environments across any sleep routine and sleep pattern. It's important to remember what is calming and why.

Sleep Routines that Can Help Calm Babies

Keep babies close

Keeping babies close helps in shared breathing, touch, warmth, and awareness of any difficulties. Babies are generally much calmer and sleep more easily if they are sleeping with their caregivers, or in very close proximity.

Babies can benefit from the shared breathing (and general sensory exchanges) with the caregiver including skin-to-skin contact, and this can be achieved to varying degrees depending on the overall safety conditions, including keeping the infant on a separate surface next to your bed, a behavior called separate-surface *co-sleeping*.

Many breastfeeding mothers find that intermittent *bedsharing* helps them continue breastfeeding, especially if they work during the day. Bedsharing (while the American Academy of Pediatrics currently recommends against it) not only increases sleep time both for mothers and babies, but has the effect of increasing the chances that mothers will breastfeed for a greater number of months than if they place their infant elsewhere for sleep.

Close proximity usually means night feeds are much easier, there are more of them, and they are far less disruptive for parents and infants, and thus can be more settling. That said, just as with any sleep arrangement, bedsharing does carry risks (as does sleeping away from the baby), and there are very clear circumstances that we know that make bedsharing not advisable.

When bedsharing should be avoided

Bedsharing should be avoided if mothers smoked during pregnancy, because infant arousal patterns may not be as efficient as they should be for maximum safety in a bedsharing environment. The same holds true for small premature infants. They are safest sleeping alongside the bed in a different sleep structure rather than in the bed. And, finally, it is highly risky to fall asleep with an infant on a couch, sofa, or armchair, as many infants have suffocated by being trapped between the adult and some part of the furniture. In all these cases, co-sleeping (different surface, same room) is more advisable than bedsharing. In any sleep location, infants must be placed on their backs to sleep.

It is important for the caregivers to refrain from bedsharing if they are not breastfeeding, and obviously if any adult is under the influence of alcohol, drugs, or anything that may impair their natural arousal patterns. Surely, babies should sleep alongside the bed on a different surface: (a) if adult bedsharers are excessively sleepy, (b) if smaller children are likely to find their way into the parents' bed, or (c) if there is another adult present in bed who refuses to take any responsibility for the infant.

Finally, wherever infants sleep they should always be placed on their backs. Moreover, if sleeping with or away from caregivers, infants should be positioned away from soft bedding, pillows, or toys and be situated so that breathing is never obstructed, with their heads never covered.

Breastfeed

In addition to all its other associated benefits to infant health and cognitive development, breastfeeding is an excellent way to calm a baby. It provides skin-to-skin contact and warmth. Breastfeeding can be of benefit to the caregiver as well, making wakings easier to manage and helping to reduce postpartum depression (Dennis & McQueen, 2009; Fergerson, Jamieson, & Lindsay, 2002; Kendall-Tackett, 2007).

In one recent study, mothers who exclusively breastfed actually got more sleep and were less tired during the day than mothers who either exclusively formula fed or both breast-and formula-fed (Kendall-Tackett, Cong, & Hale, 2011, this volume).

Listen to the baby and trust your caring instincts

Babies are master communicators, just as adults typically are masters at figuring out how best to respond. Adults don't learn to rock a baby or to talk softly…these come naturally. So to calm babies, it is helpful to follow the baby's lead and follow one's heart. Parents need to learn to follow their hearts and keep babies safe and healthy. If holding the baby seems to cause distress, then parents can stay with them, but place them in a position that seems more helpful. If the parent is still, perhaps walk; if the parent is already moving, perhaps rock. Parents should trust their instincts in how to be present with the baby.

What If the Routine Is Still Stressful?

A time may come when a parent starts thinking, "I've been doing nighttime comforting for quite awhile now. Is there anything I can do to move towards getting some uninterrupted nights?"

The answer is yes. Partly, it comes with time— varying times for different babies as Weinraub's recent study showed. And there are some things parents can do to gently move in that direction with the baby. We will share some ways to help babies need less attention at night, if that is something that is essential for a family's well-being. These approaches will build on the essential steps for calming discussed here:

Listen to the baby's signals.

Provide nurturance and support.

Help babies help themselves calm.

Remember, there is only one expert in caring for your baby—you. Sometimes you will find a way to calm your baby easily. Sometimes it may seem like what worked before doesn't work now. Being patient with your baby and yourself will help you both learn and grow.

References

Cassidy, J. (1994).Emotion regulation: Influences of attachment relationships. *Monographs of the Society for Research in Child Development,* 59, 228-283.

Davidov, M. & Grusec, J.E. (2006). Untangling the links of parental responsiveness to distress and warmth to child outcomes. *Child Development, 77,* 44-58.

Dennis, C.-L., & McQueen, K. (2009). The relationship between infant-feeding outcomes and postpartum depression: A qualitative systematic review. *Pediatrics, 123,* e736-e751.

Fergerson, S.S., Jamieson, D.J., & Lindsay, M.(2002). Diagnosing postpartum depression: Can we do better? *American Journal of Obstetrics and Gynecology,* 186, 899-902.

Hunziker, U.A., & Barr, R.G. (1986). Increased carrying reduces infant crying: A randomized controlled trial. *Pediatrics, 77,* 641-648. ftp://urstm.com/CharestJ/Articles.pdf/Hunziker%20U%201986.pdf

Kendall-Tackett, K. A. (2007). A new paradigm for depression in new mothers: The central role of inflammation and how breastfeeding and anti-inflammatory treatments protect maternal mental health. *International Breastfeeding Journal, 2:6* http://www.internationalbreastfeedingjournal.com/content/2/1/6

Kendall-Tackett, K.A., Cong, Z., & Hale, T.W. (2011). The effect of feeding method on sleep duration, maternal well-being, and postpartum depression. *Clinical Lactation, 2(2),* 22-26.

Mao, A., Burnham, M.M., Goodlin-Jones, B.L., Gaylor, E.E., & Anders T.F. (2004). A comparison of the sleep-wake patterns of cosleeping and solitary-sleeping infants. *Child Psychiatry and Human Development,* 35, 95-105.

McKenna, J.J. (1995). The potential benefits of infant-parent co-sleeping in relation to SIDS prevention, In T. O. Rognum (Ed.), *Sudden Infant Death Syndrome: New Trends in the Nineties* (pp. 257-265). Oslo, Norway: Scandinavian Press.

McKenna, J.J., & Mosko, S. (1990). Evolution and the sudden infant death syndrome (SIDS) Part II: Why human infants? *Human Nature, 1* (2), 145-177.

McKenna, J.J., & Mosko, S. (1990). Evolution and the sudden infant death syndrome (SIDS), Part III: Parent-infant co-sleeping and infant arousal, *Human Nature, 1*(2), 145-177.

McKenna, J.J., & Mosko, S. (2001). Mother-infant cosleeping: Toward a new scientific beginning. In R. Byard & H. Krous, (Eds.), *Sudden Infant Death Syndrome: Puzzles, problems and possibilities.* London: Arnold Publishers.

Mosko, S., Richard, C., & McKenna, J. (1997). Infant arousals during mother-infant bed sharing: Implications for infant Ssleep and SIDS research. *Pediatrics, 100*(2), 841-849.

Mosko, S., Richard, C., & McKenna, J. (1997). Maternal sleep and arousals during bedsharing with infants. *Sleep, 201*(2), 142-150.

Stifter, C.A., & Spinrad, T.L. (2002). The effect of excessive crying on the development of emotion regulation. *Infancy, 3*, 133-152.

Weinraub, M., Bender, R.H., Friedman, S.L., Susman, E.J., Knoke, B., Bradley, R., Houts, R., Williams, J. (2012). Patterns of developmental change in infants' nighttime sleep awakenings from 6 through 36 months of age. *Developmental Psychology, 48*, 1501-1528.

Reprinted from a Praeclarus Press White Paper: *Simple Ways to Calm a Crying Baby*. A free download of this White Paper is available from Praeclarus Press (www. PraeclarusPress.com). Used with permission.

Author Biographies

Helen Ball, Ph.D., is Head of Anthropology at Durham University, UK, Director of the Parent-Infant Sleep Lab, and Fellow of the Wolfson Institute for Health and Wellbeing. She has been researching infant sleep issues for 18 years and her work is used in safe sleep guidelines in the UK and around the world. In 2013 she was a recipient of an "Outstanding Impact in Society" award for her research by the UK Economic and Social Research Council.

Tracy Cassels, M.A., is a graduate student completing her Ph.D. in Developmental Psychology at the University of British Columbia and the founder of EvolutionaryParenting.com. She obtained her B.A. in Cognitive Science from the University of California, Berkeley and her M.A. in Clinical Psychology from the University of British Columbia. She lives in Vancouver, BC, Canada with her husband Brian, daughter Madeleine (Maddy), and stepson Desmond.

Michael Lamport Commons, Ph.D., is currently an Assistant Clinical Professor, Department of Psychiatry at Beth Israel Deaconess Medical Center, Harvard Medical School. There and as director of the Dare Institute, Cambridge, MA, he directs research relating to development and behavioral science in general.

Zhen Cong, Ph.D., is an Assistant Professor in the Department of Human Development and Family Studies at Texas Tech University in Lubbock, Texas . Her research interests include diversity in aging, migration, the well-being of the elderly and their family members, and intergenerational relations.

Thomas Hale, Ph.D., is a clinical pharmacologist, professor at Texas Tech University School of Medicine, and author of *Medications and Mothers' Milk*. He is an expert on the use of medications in breastfeeding women, and he has traveled the world lecturing on this topic. He is considered one of the leading experts in the field of human lactation and the use of medication.

John Hoffman is the married father of three young men. He has spent more than 20 years as a regular writer for a Canadian magazine called *Today's Parent*. He has written features on various aspects of parenting, specializing in fathering, sleep, children's mental health, education and, more recently autism and self-regulation. He now splits his time between freelance writing and working as a contract research associate for the Milton and Ethel Harris Research Institute, based at York University in Toronto, Ontario.

Kathleen Kendall-Tackett, Ph.D., IBCLC, RLC, FAPA, is a health psychologist, IBCLC, Fellow of the American Psychological Association, and is President-Elect of APA's Division of Trauma Psychology. Dr. Kendall-Tackett is Editor-in-Chief of *Clinical Lactation* and owner of Praeclarus Press. Dr. Kendall-Tackett is the author or editor of 23 books and 360 articles or chapters on maternal depression, trauma, women's health, and breastfeeding. She is co-principal investigator of the Survey of Mothers' Sleep and Fatigue, which won the John Kennell and Marshall Klaus Award for Excellence in Research from DONA International in 2011.

James McKenna, Ph.D., is recognized as the world's leading authority on mother-infant co-sleeping, in relationship to breastfeeding and SIDS. In recognition of his work in 2009 he was admitted as a Fellow into the select body of the American Association for the Advancement of Science. That same year and in recognition of his extensive work with television, radio, and print media he received from the American Anthropological Association the "2008 Anthropology In The Media Award," an award presented to anthropologists by the association in recognition of his distinguished work in educating the public to the importance of anthropological concepts.

Wendy Middlemiss, Ph.D., CFLE, is Associate Professor of Educational Psychology at the University of North Texas. Her work encompasses research examining the effect of different childrearing approaches and exploring how to share this information with families and communities to promote infant, child, and family health.

Patrice Marie Miller, Ed.D., is a Professor in the Department of Psychology at Salem State University, and Lecturer at Harvard Medical School. Her research on the cognitive, social, and emotional development of individuals focuses on the influence of early experiences, parenting, socioeconomic background, and culture.

Darcia Narvaez, Ph.D., is an Associate Professor of Psychology, and Director of the Collaborative for Ethical Education at the University of Notre Dame. Her research explores questions of moral cognition, moral development, and moral character education. She has developed several integrative theories: Adaptive Ethical Expertise, Integrative Ethical Education, and Triune Ethics Theory. She spoke at the White House's conference on Character and Community. She is author or editor of three award-winning books: *Postconventional Moral Thinking; Moral Development, Self and Identity;* and *The Handbook of Moral and Character Education.*

Sarah Ockwell-Smith holds a first degree in Psychology, and spent several years working in pharmaceutical research and development. After the birth of her firstborn she retrained as a Doula, Antenatal Teacher, Baby Massage Instructor, Homeopath and Hypnotherapist. She is the founder of BabyCalm and ToddlerCalm Ltd, and author of books of the same name. Sarah lives with her husband and four school-aged children close to Cambridge, England.

Helen Stevens is a registered nurse, midwife, maternal & child health nurse, with a B. App Science and training in Family Partnerships Model and Circle of a Security. She has 15 years' experience in early parenting. As author of the *Safe Sleep Space,* and co-author of subsequent *Safe Sleep Space* DVDs and RockaBub app, she has been supporting families around the world in responding to babies and children at sleep time. Helen lives with her family in Melbourne, Australia.

Made in the USA
San Bernardino, CA
16 February 2016